The Million Dollar Machine®
Life Skills Enrichment Program
Grades K-3

For Educators, Mentors and Parents

By Kent Davis

In Consultation With:

David P. GoWell
Original Curriculum Co-Author

Steven P. Schinke, Ph.D.
Professor, School of Social Work
Columbia University

Steven W. Godin, Ph.D.
Coordinator of Program Evaluation and Research
University of Medicine and Dentistry of New Jersey

H. James Wasser, M.A.
Substance Abuse Prevention Specialist

Michelle Parker Rock, M.S. Ed.
Elementary Curriculum Specialist

Micki McKisson, M.A.
Environmental Education Consultant
Greenpeace North American Education Coordinator

Featuring Illustrations by Donald G. O'Brien

www.LifeSkills4Kids.com

The MDM Life Skills Lesson Collection

The complete Million Dollar Machine lesson collection includes more than 1,200 integrated activities, 80 interactive worksheets, vocabulary and full implementation guidelines. Lessons are available in four convenient formats at www.LifeSkills4Kids.com:

Print Edition: Grades K-3 and Grades 4-6

These convenient printed lesson collections give you instant access to all the lessons without a computer. Also available on Amazon.com.

Instant Digital Download: Grades K-3 and Grades 4-6

Download the complete collection directly to your computer including printable PDF lessons with URL links to help you plan exercises and activities.

NEW! DVD Gift Pack

A great gift for teachers, mentors, youth group leaders and parents. The DVD includes the complete Grade K-3 and 4-6 lesson collections in printable PDF format with helpful Internet links to plan exercises and activities. The DVD also includes more than 150 Wikipedia background articles for offline reference use.

MDM School Assembly Program with Robot Teacher!

Give your students an unforgettable learning experience by inviting our robot teacher to your school. Scheduled on a district level the cost is as low as $3 per student, including MDM lesson plans for teachers to use throughout the school year. Call **800-262-2162** to learn more.

DatAsia, Inc.

Published by DatAsia, Inc. Holmes Beach, FL 34218

© Copyright 2008 - RoboMedia, Inc., 12 Phillips Rd, Hainesport, NJ 08036 TEL: 609-261-2162

All rights reserved. No part of this book may be reproduced, stored in a retrieval system, or transmitted in any form without prior permission.

Educators and parents who purchase the lessons in book, DVD or downloadable PDF form are granted a limited license to reproduce worksheets for their students and children.

"Million Dollar Machine®" is a registered trademark of RoboMedia, Inc., Hainesport, NJ 08036.

ISBN: 978-1-934431-57-3
Library of Congress Preassigned Control Number: 2008901783

Table of Contents

The Million Dollar Machine Cheer 4
Welcome Educators, Mentors and Parents 5
Introduction to the Lessons 6
How to Use Your MDM Lessons Effectively 9
Tips for Using MDM in the Classroom 12

Self Awareness

1. I love myself because I'm special. 14
2. It's OK to have different feelings. 18
3. I take care of my body because it's the most valuable thing I'll ever own. 22
4. I'll grow up to be my best if I take care of my body. 26

Interpersonal Skills

5. Everyone I meet is special. 30
6. I respect other people. 34
7. I use teamwork when I work and play with other people. 38
8. I am a good friend. 42
9. I'm an important part of my family. 46

Decision Making

10. I make important decisions for myself every day. 50
11. I know ways to solve many of my own problems. 54
12. I stand up for myself when people tell me to do bad things. 58
13. I know who to go to when I need help. 62

Drug Awareness

14. I must protect my body from dangerous things. 66
15. Cigarettes, alcohol and other drugs damage the body. 70
16. Only a doctor or my parents can give me medicine. 74
17. It's not my fault if someone I love uses tobacco, alcohol or other drugs. 78

Earth Skills

18. I love my planet because it's special. 82
19. I'm an important member of nature's team. 86
20. I will control my planet's future. 90

Vocabulary 94
Online Learning Resources 96
Million Dollar Machine Fact Sheet 98

The Million Dollar Machine Cheer

Lesson Note: In schools, a sophisticated robot teacher can introduce all 20 Learning Objectives to your students with a live special assembly show. This dynamic presentation emphasizes how extra-ordinary the human body is using concrete examples children understand. **As the robot teaches, the children soon learn that he is <u>not</u> the "*Million Dollar Machine*" the program is named for; <u>they are!</u>**

This high-energy learning experience gives children an unforgettable introduction to the life skills concepts in these lessons, making it easier for teachers and parents to generate excitement for the activities throughout the school year. The cheer below is one part of the assembly.

Who's the Million Dollar Machine?
ME!
How many Million Dollar Machines do you get?
ONE!
Who controls your Million Dollar Machine?
ME!
If someone wants you to hurt your body, what are you going to say?
NO WAY!
Are you gonna keep a clean machine?
YES!
You kids are the greatest!
Remember, you and your Million Dollar Machine can accomplish anything!

This energetic cheer summarizes key MDM learning objectives,
reinforces children's self-esteem and membership in the class team.

Welcome Educators, Mentors and Parents!

Dear Educators, Mentors and Parents,

Welcome to the revised 2009 edition of the Million Dollar Machine (MDM) program.

This comprehensive lesson collection will help you guide your children to achieving their personal best in life. Best of all, this proven format makes it easy and fun for you and your children to learn and grow together.

Over the last twenty years, it has been a privilege to create and refine these activities with expert educators, classroom teachers, parents and students throughout the United States. This personal, hands-on effort has been a major factor in making the MDM lessons so effective and easy to use.

This edition includes all the field-tested, scientifically validated exercises of the original school-based curriculum. Parent-child learning has always been a vital component of our life skills education approach. With this revised edition, MDM is even more accessible to parents, allowing them to share all these simple, yet profound, learning activities with their children.

You can begin using these lessons with your children immediately after reviewing the concise introduction and guidelines that follow. A special section gives teachers additional suggestions for classroom implementation. To help teachers and parents gather additional information we also include suggested Internet links using Wikipedia, Google and other on-line resources.

Following the introduction, there are 20 learning objectives, hundreds of activities in three different learning styles, 40 interactive child-parent worksheets, and vocabulary suggestions at the end of the book. Finally, you'll find information about our award-winning life skills school assembly program, that an unforgettable robot teacher actually presents right in your school!

I personally wish each of you tremendous success, in using these lessons and in helping your children to grow up to be their best.

Sincerely,

Kent Davis
MDM Author & 2009 Revision Editor

Introduction to the Lessons

What are the MDM program's objectives?

The Million Dollar Machine (MDM) program gives children a broad range of positive skills with far-reaching benefits. For more than 20 years, classroom educators have used this program for Character Education, Health Education and Drug Use Prevention. As you'll discover, MDM's holistic life skills approach fulfills these educational needs and many more.

The MDM lessons give children the essential knowledge and skills they need to take responsibility for their lives and to reach their full potential. This comprehensive program was specially designed to help your children in every area of personal and academic life by:

- **increasing self-esteem and self-responsibility,**
- **strengthening relationships between children and caregivers,**
- **inspiring good nutrition, fitness, hygiene and other healthy behaviors**
- **developing positive social skills,**
- **developing critical thinking and decision making skills,**
- **training children to protect themselves from drugs and other harmful influences,**
- **inspiring children to stay in school and develop a lifetime enthusiasm for learning, and**
- **empowering children to take charge of themselves and our planet's future.**

MDM has always emphasized parental involvement as a vital part of every child's education. This new edition empowers home caregivers even more, giving them all the professional teaching tools they need to create and share life skills learning experiences with their children.

How were the MDM lessons developed?

In 1987, teachers and parents nationwide were seeking effective ways to instill positive health skills in children and to prevent drug use. To meet that need, MDM authors Kent Davis and David GoWell designed an interactive school-based group presentation. To make the health concepts powerful and unforgettable for children, they invented a dynamic multi-media robot teacher to present the entire show, teaching children that their bodies are the miraculous "million dollar machines" for which the program is named.

The next challenge was creating an effective curriculum so teachers and parents could reinforce the life skills lessons throughout the school year. In consultation with educators, psychologists and drug use prevention experts, the authors reviewed curricula from 19 states before organizing the concepts included in the original MDM lessons. With help from corporate and private grants, the development team monitored hundreds of live presentations over a two year period, working with classroom teachers evaluating content and teaching techniques as well as student comprehension and retention.

More than 450,000 children participated in the Million Dollar Machine pilot programs. This comprehensive, powerful and easy-to-use MDM lesson collection is the result of that field experience. The robot assembly presentations continue to fascinate children nationwide; more than 3,000,000 children have now experienced the excitement of an MDM school assembly.

Today, children still urgently need the guidance that life skills education provides. In 2007, a trial program gave teachers and parents direct Internet access to the MDM lessons for the first time. Their positive feedback, and the demand for effective life skills training, inspired this revised edition of the Million Dollar Machine lesson collection for teachers and parents worldwide.

Introduction to the Lessons

What skills will your children gain from these lessons?

This lesson collection for Grades K-3 covers 20 Learning Objectives in five areas:

Self Awareness

Self Awareness lessons help children discover that their bodies are priceless, irreplaceable "million dollar machines" that allow them to accomplish their dreams. These activities demonstrate the priceless and irreplaceable nature of the human body, appropriate ways to deal with feelings, personal health and hygiene skills and an introduction to setting and attaining goals in life.

Interpersonal Skills

Interpersonal Skills develop children's ability to interact with others and to work in groups. By understanding the special qualities in others, these lessons develop empathy, courtesy, friendship, cooperation and teamwork. The section ends by establishing the special role children have as family members.

Decision Making

Decision Making is one of the most important skills in life. A simple problem solving model is presented, with numerous opportunities to practice using it at home and at school. These lessons improve responsibility skills and confidence by teaching children to deal with decisions and problems. Finally, a series of activities help children learn how to rely on trusted adults for help with problems.

Drug Awareness

Drug Awareness addresses alcohol, tobacco and other drugs as visible and highly accessible threats to children. The lessons focus on tobacco and alcohol use because those drugs are the first children are likely to encounter. Rather than dwelling on detailed drug information, children learn why they should avoid using any drug at any time. The lessons give a full understanding of medicine as a healing tool used by trained professionals. Social and family problems caused by drugs, and how children can deal with them, are also explored.

Earth Skills

Earth Skills give children a clear perspective of themselves in relation to the planet and the environment around them. By establishing Earth as a priceless, irreplaceable resource that all living beings share, children become dynamic participants in the natural world around them. In addition to imparting intellectual understanding of these concepts, this section includes pro-active activities that directly involve children in conservation projects and positive environmental behaviors.

Introduction to the Lessons

Are the MDM lessons suitable for home schooling?

Absolutely. MDM was developed in formal school environments by professional educators. MDM's teaching techniques were refined and used in classroom situations for the program's first twenty years. Now, all parents can benefit using these lessons and activities at home. Home schooling parents have the additional opportunity of incorporating aspects of this program into many areas of their ongoing curriculum. In the Classroom Section you'll find more information about how to use MDM as an "integrated curriculum."

How are MDM lessons different from "Just Say No"?

"Just Say No" was popularized by government agencies in the 80's as an attempt to control drug use. This simplistic and ineffective approach frustrated professional educators who knew that children needed far more than a three word order to stop them from using drugs. Teachers and parents also knew that children must begin acquiring health and thinking skills at a very young age so that they are prepared by the time they must confront life threatening decisions. Fortunately, the federal government agreed, and introduced mandatory drug prevention education in schools. This law created the opportunity to develop and refine the innovative life skills teaching techniques used in the Million Dollar Machine lessons.

MDM's approach is to inspire children to learn new things, to be their best and to accomplish their dreams. MDM is first and foremost about saying "yes" to the good things in life. Helping children realize they have unlimited potential and can control their future gives them a better perspective when they encounter negative things in life. With a positive self image, strong personal goals and good decision making skills, children naturally perceive drugs, crime and high risk behaviors as threats to their future. And, as we all know, when a child wants to say "no" *for their own reasons*, their minds are quite set!

How do MDM lessons define the term "drug"?

In these lessons, the term "drug" means any substance that is illegal and harmful for children, including alcohol and tobacco, which are legal for adults. Medicines, prescriptions and over-the-counter medications are specified as such, and are not called "drugs." MDM teaches the appropriate use of these items as healing tools used by qualified professionals.

How do the MDM lessons prevent drug use?

Scientific research indicates that developing life skills plays a vital role in preventing childhood drug use. First, MDM establishes the human body as our most priceless, irreplaceable possession. Next, MDM gives children the reasons and decision making skills they need to decide against drug use for themselves. Drugs become a threat to their well-being rather than an opportunity to "try a new experience," to "get away with something" or to "fit in." Finally, MDM gives children specific techniques they can use to escape from peer pressure and avoid dangerous situations.

Developing self-esteem and health awareness also motivates children to protect themselves in general. These self-protection concepts give children the desire and ability to resist many other dangers, such as stealing, risk-taking, violence or sexual misconduct.

How to Use Your MDM Lessons Effectively

What is the best way to use these lessons?

Regular...and relaxed. Think of this collection like a cookbook with hundreds of "recipes" to improve your child's life and health. Every recipe isn't for every teacher, parent or child. You don't have to use the lessons in any particular order for them to be effective—you just have to use them!

The variety of discussion points and activities allows you to fulfill each objective with your children in many different ways. The activities are grouped in a variety of Teaching Styles to maximize your effectiveness and your children's interest. You'll find that the exercises easily integrate with many other subjects, such as social studies, language arts, science, physical education, art and music.

Are these lessons suitable for all types of children?

Here's an interesting fact: Children (*and adults*) interpret life skills concepts at their own level of growth. The question "What makes a good friend?" is as profound to discuss for a five year old as for a fifty year old! There are often no "right" answers. The discussion itself is the learning experience and hearing other people's viewpoints expands our own understanding.

You choose the discussion points and activities that best fit your students' capabilities. In classroom environments, teachers may assign more difficult activities to advanced students, and less demanding activities to the remainder of the class. Over the past twenty years creative educators and parents have used MDM's life skills lessons successfully with a variety of students including those with special learning needs, physical challenges and even higher age groups.

How are the lessons organized?

Each of the 20 Learning Objectives has two pages of activities and two worksheets.

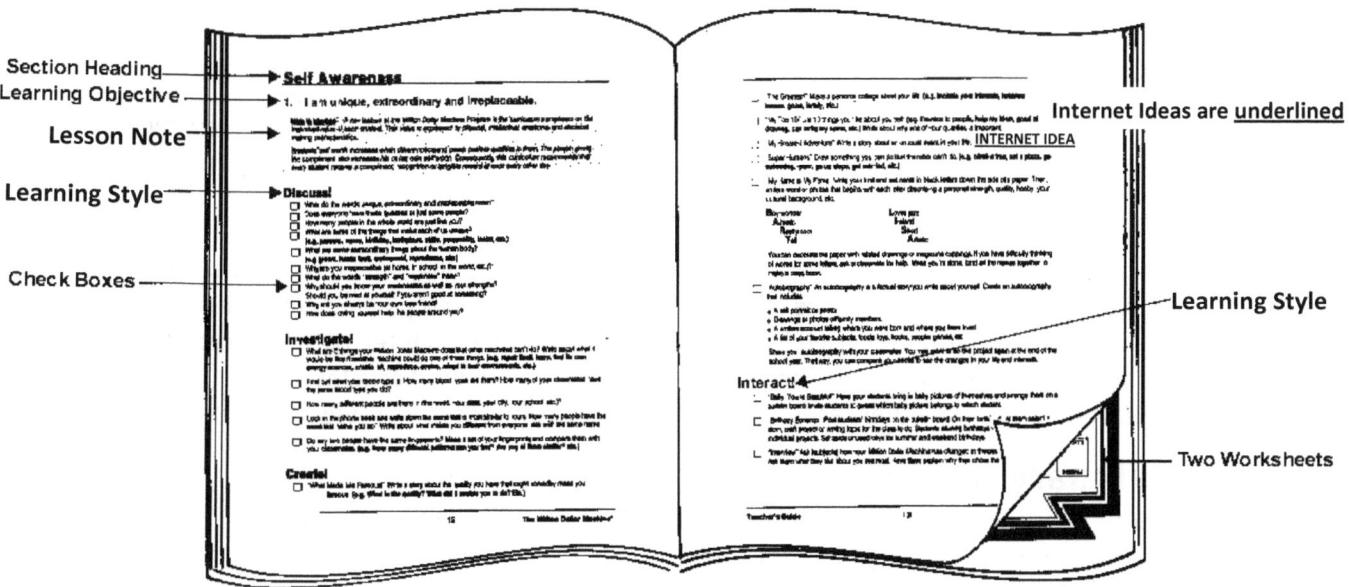

Each **Learning Objective** appears on the left page under the **Section Heading**. "**Lesson Notes**" give a brief overview. These two pages contain a wide selection of activities in a variety of **Learning Styles** so you can choose those most suited to your students and your teaching objectives. **Internet Ideas** for teacher-parent use are underlined. Boxes (☐) provide an easy check (✓) of completed exercises.

How to Use Your MDM Lessons Effectively

How do different "Learning Styles" help?

Every teacher, parent and child teaches and learns in different ways. The MDM lessons use a variety of styles to help you and your children explore and retain the material most effectively:

Talk!

Your most powerful teaching tool is simply *talking*. The discussion questions are specifically designed to build a complete foundation for each Learning Objective. Answers are suggested for fact-based questions but most questions allow children to explore their own feelings and opinions. The discussion points make it easy for teachers and parents to guide conversations. In most cases, your children will teach themselves and their classmates.

Make!

This style develops imagination and self-expression using artistic themes. Most activities are presented as art or craft projects. If you wish, you can adapt many as poetry, music or even simple written projects for older children. Occasionally, you can allow students to pick their own means of expression.

Play!

This style develops communication and interactive skills both inside and outside the classroom. Many activities involve role play or other types of group participation. Sometimes, a field trip is suggested. "**Visitor**" activities are also included under this heading.

"**Visitor**" activities recommend special guests you can invite to speak to your class. Parents and local professional organizations are good sources of speakers. Be sure to explain the Learning Objective and the goal of your lesson to each visitor in advance.

Child-Parent Worksheets

Each Learning Objective has two dedicated worksheets for children to complete and review with their parents. For school use, worksheets have a Parent's Initial box to check parental participation.

Internet Ideas

Children acquire life skills most effectively from interactive learning, which is why MDM emphasizes traditional methods like talking, artistic expression and playing with others. For teachers and parents, these revised lessons also include suggested Internet resources for additional information. Underlined terms in the text refer to helpful articles at www.Wikipedia.org. For other resources, full Internet addresses are provided.

Vocabulary

A list of ten vocabulary words for each Learning Objective appears after the lessons. Use these words in your regular language arts and spelling lessons.

How to Use Your MDM Lessons Effectively

Why are discussions so important?

It's amazing that something as simple as a good conversation is so effective as a teaching tool! Scientific research demonstrates that children have an innate knowledge of life skills. Your guided discussions will draw that knowledge out. This interrogatory style of teaching is called the "the Socratic method." Research and experience show that the Socratic method maximizes comprehension and participation. The Socratic method is particularly beneficial for children who rarely take part in classroom or family discussions.

Student-teacher and child-parent interaction are vital components of every MDM Learning Objective. Covering the "Talk!" questions first gives your children an excellent grasp of each concept. This is important preparation for completing the rest of the activities and worksheets.

Encouraging children to share personal experiences promotes the free exchange of information, ideas and feelings. With your guidance, children will suggest most of the appropriate answers themselves. As discussion leader, you should act as the expert or final authority on the subject only after you feel your children have exhausted their own ideas.

How can I maintain the excitement of these lessons?

Here are a few guidelines to help you:

- **Be regular!** Schedule a daily or weekly "Million Dollar Machine Time" to use these lessons. Scientific evidence demonstrates that life skills curricula are more effective when presented over an extended period of time.
- **Be flexible!** You may choose to explore some of the Learning Objectives on a purely verbal level. Just a few minutes of discussion or role play will accomplish a great deal. You can also use the worksheets to save time on written assignments.
- **Share!** Get together with other teachers or parents to exchange ideas on activities that were particularly effective.
- **Take it easy!** Having your students teach each other will make these lessons even more effective. Children are more likely to adopt positive attitudes and good morals from their peers than they are from teachers and parents.
- **Integrate!** This program will benefit your children in every area of their lives. You can easily combine these activities with your regular social studies, sports, language arts, science, art and music lessons.
- **Innovate!** Using the MDM lesson examples, you'll quickly understand how to build positive life skills into nearly every learning activity. The suggested Internet resources will help you expand on your ideas.
- **Have fun!** These lessons convey essential skills that everyone needs to succeed in life. The activities and worksheets in this lesson collection were designed to give you a variety of ways to share these important lessons with your children. Just like thousands of teachers, mentors and parents around the world, you'll discover that the Million Dollar Machine lessons are easy to use and fun. And most important: they work.

Tips for Using MDM in the Classroom

How will I find time to use the MDM lessons?

Here's a gift from the teachers in the 1980's to you in the New Millennium! A key factor that influenced MDM's development was the US federal government's Anti-Drug Abuse Act of 1986, which required mandatory drug prevention education in all schools. However, this positive step instantly created a huge additional burden for teachers: where would they find the additional classroom hours to meet the requirements? To make matters worse, where would they find the time for additional in-service training to qualify them to teach this additional mandated subject matter?

One solution was to use "integrated" life skills training as part of existing curricula. Life skills education offers a holistic approach to addressing the drug problem, giving children the skills *and motivation* they need to avoid drugs. Because most children have an innate understanding of life skills (e.g. What is a good friend? Why should I take care of my body? Who decides my future?) teachers didn't require extensive training to introduce these concepts.

Moreover, teachers who participated in developing the MDM lessons worked to integrate them into existing subjects. So, MDM's life skills concepts can easily become part of other mandated curricula such as math, science, language arts, social studies, physical fitness, health education, etc.

In conclusion, MDM won't take time away from the other subjects that you must cover. MDM simply gives you the opportunity to include life skills exercises in those subjects. This is why the educators developing MDM included so many activities and learning styles. The object is not to do them all—the object is to give you a great selection so you can find exercises that fit your particular teaching needs.

What is the importance of small group activities?

Small group activities develop social skills, leadership skills, and self-motivation. When organizing groups, divide your class in different ways to avoid always having the same students together **(e.g. alphabetically, by height, by random drawing, by seating, etc.).** Ask each group to appoint a responsible leader to maintain order.

Some students may have difficulty participating in a productive manner. Give these students the extra responsibility of leading a group or place these students in a group under your direct supervision. By doing so, you can engage all of your students in a constructive small group experience.

What is the importance of role play activities?

Role playing is the most effective way to develop interactive skills. Students must think, feel and act, responding totally to each dramatic situation. Role play also gives your students the opportunity to act out real-life situations and practice refusal skills and problem-solving techniques.

Here are a few ideas to strengthen your role play activities:

- Tell different groups of students to play the same scene.
- Repeat a role play after having students exchange roles.
- Use props and costumes to add realism or humor.
- Use sound, scenery or lighting effects to add drama.
- Ask your students to perform their best skits for another class.
- Record performances on video to play back for students, parents and other classes.
- Ask students in the audience to write down alternative responses.
- Praise students for their performance and participation.

Tips for Using MDM in the Classroom

How do parents make these lessons more effective?

Parental involvement is essential for successful life skills development. That's why this lesson collection includes a number of teaching activities to increase child-parent interaction.

1. Use the worksheets accompanying each Learning Objective so students can practice their life skills at home. The worksheets provide an ideal time for parents to share structured teaching activities with their children. Initial boxes are provided to verify parental participation. The worksheets also stimulate family interest and discussions on important topics.

2. Designate parents as the primary subjects when you assign the "**Interview!**" activities. These interviews give parents a structured way to share their experiences, and participate in their child's education. Interviews also facilitate child-family communication, increasing the confidence and self-esteem of everyone involved.

3. Invite parents to be "**Visitors**" whenever possible. Your students' parents have a variety of diverse careers, skills, talents, hobbies, travel experiences and cultural backgrounds. Once a few parents participate, others will want to contribute as well.

How does the robot assembly help children learn?

The Million Dollar Machine special assembly program gives teachers and parents a memorable reference point that reinforces all the life skills concepts in these lessons. To read educator comments about the assembly please visit the Program Validation section at LifeSkills4Kids.com

In each assembly, a dynamic multi-media robot teacher introduces all 20 life skills learning objectives, conducting the entire 35-40 minute assembly for groups of up to 250 students. Today's children are inundated with all types of entertainment devices and movies are filled with amazing special effects. Introducing these health skills with an interactive robot in your school is an attention getting special effect that captivates children and evens the playing field between schools and the outside world.

Student retention of the robot's presentation is excellent. Following the assembly, teachers receive the age appropriate lesson collections to reinforce and expand on the concepts throughout the school year. Many districts also add "Parent's Night" events to the assembly schedules so that children can bring their parents to school to meet the amazing robot teacher.

Scheduled on a district basis, MDM assemblies are quite economical. With an effective tour itinerary the cost can be as low as $3 per student, *including* the complete MDM lessons for every teacher.

How can my school get the MDM assembly free?

Often, all you have to do is ask a potential sponsor! Since 1986, public-spirited organizations, corporations and individuals have funded more than 60% of all MDM assembly programs. Just call us at 800-262-2162 for ideas and support in seeking funding.

Every robot-taught assembly is a high-visibility local event that can attract the type of positive media attention that sponsors love. Local companies and organizations have literally sponsored thousands of shows for schools or subsidized travel expenses.

Groups that have funded our educational programs include PTAs and PTOs; health care providers; local companies like banks, hotels, restaurants and hospitals; national corporations with a local presence; civic organizations (Lions, Rotary), and many others.

Self Awareness

1. I love myself because I'm special.

Lesson Notes: A key concept of the Million Dollar Machine curriculum is emphasizing the individual value of each child and making this value *tangible*. Many of the lessons and activities help children appreciate their own capabilities and the physical and intellectual attributes that make them unique.

A child's self worth increases when they examine and understand positive qualities within themselves. When other people compliment a child on special qualities it also increases his or her own self-confidence and self-worth. We recommend that every child receives a compliment, recognition or tangible reward for positive behavior every day.

Talk

- ☐ What does "**special**" mean to you?
- ☐ Is everyone special or are just some people special?
- ☐ Why is it important to love yourself? Why is it important for you to take care of yourself?
- ☐ How many people in the whole world are just like you?
- ☐ What are some of the things that make each of us special?
  (e.g. parents, name, birthday, birthplace, skills, friendliness, looks, etc.)
- ☐ What do the words "**strength**" and "**weakness**" mean?
- ☐ Why should you know your weaknesses as well as your strengths?
- ☐ Should you be mad at yourself if you aren't good at something? What else can you do?
- ☐ Why will you always be your own best friend?
- ☐ How does loving yourself help the people around you?

Make

- ☐ **"Why I'm Great!"** Have your students draw their names with fancy letters and list 5 things they like about themselves around the edges. (e.g. I'm nice to people, help my mom, good at drawing, can write my name, etc.)
- ☐ **"Personal Snowflake"** Have each child cut out a big paper snowflake. Explain that no two snowflakes are exactly alike, just as no two people are exactly alike. Then, have them write words that describe themselves on the points of the snowflake.
- ☐ **"What's in Your Name Game!"** Have children write their names in block letters down the side of a paper. Then, have them write a word or phrase for each letter. Encourage them to write words describing personal strengths, qualities, hobbies, cultural background, etc. Decorate the papers with drawings or pictures. Older children can do their last names, too.
  Do examples on the chalkboard to get them started:

T rustworthy	**E** nthusiastic	**B** aseball
I mportant	**D** evoted reader	**R** eliable
N ice person	**D** enmark	**A** thlete
A rtistic	**Y** oung	**D** ynamic

Self Awareness

- ☐ **"All About Me!"** Have students create a book about themselves including:
    - A self portrait or photo
    - Drawings or photos of family members
    - Lists and drawings of things the child likes about school
    - Drawings or photos of favorite foods, toys, books, people, games, etc.

    Once the pages are finished, bind each book by stapling them together. Set aside a special shelf in the room for the students' books. Ask children to share their **"All About Me"** books with the class. Explain that each book is different because each person is unique.

- ☐ **Idea:** Do this project *again* at the end of the school year. Your students can compare the two books to see the changes in their lives and interests.

- ☐ **"Do Well. Do Better!"** Have your children draw pictures of something they do well and something they do not do well. Ask for volunteers to talk about their pictures. The class can offer suggestions on how to improve each other's abilities.

- ☐ **"My Special Quality"** Have your children draw pictures of their most special quality. Ask for volunteers to talk about their pictures. **(e.g. being able to run fast, having a nice smile, playing a musical instrument, etc.)**

Play

- ☐ **"Today's My Day"** Post students' birthdays on the bulletin board. On their birthdays, let them select a craft project or story for the class from options you provide. Children sharing birthdays should contribute individual projects. Set aside special days for summer and weekend birthdays.

- ☐ **"Guess Who?"** Each week, prepare a list of physical qualities and positive characteristics describing one of your students. Read these to the class and have children guess who you're describing. Explain why you picked those qualities to describe the child.

- ☐ **"Citizen of the Week"** Start a program recognizing students for non-academic, positive behavior. **(e.g. good citizenship, politeness, cheerfulness, achieving a goal, helpfulness, attention to rules, etc.)** Students and teachers can take part in the selection process.
    The "Citizen of the Week" should receive some extra attention, for example:
    - a badge proclaiming him or her as "Citizen of the Week"
    - becoming special monitor or helper for the week
    - being allowed to help choose a craft project for the class to do
    - having his or her picture put up on a class bulletin board
    - receiving a "proclamation" describing his or her positive behavior
    - recognizing his or her "good citizen award" at a parent or school function

- ☐ **"Mirror, Mirror"** Have your students sit in a circle. As the teacher plays recorded music, the children pass around an unbreakable hand mirror. When the music stops, the child with the mirror looks into it and says, "I am special because _____," filling in the blank. The game proceeds giving everyone a turn.

All About ME!

Here are some things that make me special:

1. My **name** is _____.
2. I was **born** in_____.
3. My **eyes** are _____ and my **hair** is _____.
4. I **weigh** _____ and I'm _____ **tall**.
5. I was **born** _____ and I'm in ____ **grade**.
6. I go to _____ **School**.

Draw or glue your picture here

7. I live with _____ other people. Their names are _____.

8. My favorite **game** is _____.

9. My favorite **book** is _____.

10. My favorite **color** is _____.

11. Two things I do **really well** are:
_____

12. Two things I want **to learn to do better** are:
_____

13. Two things I like to do with my **family** are:
_____

14. Two things I like to do in **school** are:
_____

15. Two things I like to do with my **friends** are:
_____

PARENT'S INITIALS

© Copyright 2008 RoboMedia, Inc. – www.LifeSkills4Kids.com

Time Line

Name _____

Date _____

You & your Million Dollar Machine have done a lot since you were born!

★ Use this timeline to list some of your experiences and achievements, **starting at the bottom**. Write at least one for each year of your life. When you finish listing things you've already done, think about something you will learn by *next* year.

★ If you want more room, copy your timeline onto a larger piece of paper. You can add photographs, pictures from magazines or drawings too!

★ Parents, close friends and relatives are great sources for information!

My Next Experience

	Dates	**My Experiences** (below)	
When did you first go to school?	_____	_____	
Did you ever have a pet?	_____	_____	When was the first time you earned money?
When was your first trip on a plane, boat or train?	_____	_____	If you have brothers or sisters when were they born?
What's the first movie you remember seeing?	_____	_____	What is the first vacation you remember?
When did you learn to ride a bike?	_____	_____	Who was your first best friend?
What was your first favorite TV show?	_____	_____	What's the first book you read by yourself?
What is the farthest you have ever been from home?	_____	_____	How old were you when you first used a computer?
Have you ever had to go to the hospital?	_____	_____	How old were you when you learned to write?
When did you learn to walk?	_____	_____	

DATE _____ **I was born!!!** _____

City   State   Weight

| PARENT'S INITIALS | Did you ever have measles, mumps, or chicken pox? | Did you ever learn to swim? |

© Copyright 2008 RoboMedia, Inc. – www.LifeSkills4Kids.com

Self Awareness

2. It's OK to have different feelings.

> **Note to teacher:** These activities teach children that feelings are as much a part of their lives as physical characteristics. Feelings and emotions affect our body's well-being, so dealing with them appropriately actually improves health. Regardless of whether feelings are good or bad, learning to deal with them is an essential life-skill for children to master.

Talk

- ☐ How does it feel when you are: (**e.g. happy, sad, afraid, amused, angry, bored, confused, delighted, excited, frightened, great, hurt, interested, jealous, lonely, moody, normal, proud, quiet, scared, surprised, nervous, timid, upset, worried, etc.**)
- ☐ What are feelings? Are feelings good or bad? What things can cause the feelings above?
- ☐ What are some ways you express feelings? (**e.g. facial expressions, hugs, tears, words, pictures, gifts, etc.**)
- ☐ Can you tell how someone is feeling by the way they act?
- ☐ Do other people have feelings like yours?
- ☐ What are some things that make people feel mixed up or confused?
- ☐ What are some things that upset people? Does being upset affect your whole body?
- ☐ How does it make your (**eyes, head, heart, stomach, skin**) feel?
- ☐ What would happen if we hid our feelings all the time?
- ☐ Why is it important to let people know how we feel?
- ☐ Should we sometimes keep our feelings to ourselves?
- ☐ Why should you talk to a trusted adult about strong feelings?

Make

- ☐ **"Dealing With Feeling"** Explain that it's normal to have all kinds of feelings, good and bad. Good feelings can be shared. Some activities can make bad feelings go away. Assign a different feeling to each student. Have them draw what he or she could do to enjoy the feeling (**if it's good**) or change the feeling (**if it's bad**). (e.g. "happy" students could draw themselves hugging a parent or playing with friends, "sad" students could draw themselves talking to a friend, etc.) Have students describe their drawings to the class.
- ☐ **"Warm & Fuzzy"** Have your students name things that make them happy. Write them on the chalkboard. Have each student draw his or her favorite thing and describe how it makes him or her feel inside.
- ☐ **"Mask Makers"** Explain that sometimes people wear "masks" to hide their true feelings. They hide their feelings because they are afraid of not being accepted, being embarrassed, or because they don't know how to express their feelings. The mask might be smiling when they are really feeling sad. Have students make masks with paper plates and crayons. Punch holes in the sides of the masks and tie with yarn. Then, have students wear their masks while pretending to have different feelings (**happy, sad, angry, etc.**). Other students try to guess the feeling behind the masks. At the end, students lower the masks to show their expressions. Ask students if they have ever covered up their feelings this way. What are the benefits of letting people know how you really feel?
- ☐ **"Quiet Thoughts"** Ask your children if they ever lie in bed and think about what happened during the day. The things we think about before (or after) sleep are usually important to us. By sharing these thoughts and feelings, it's easier to be close to our family and friends.
Have the students draw a picture of something they thought about before going to sleep.

Self Awareness

- ☐ **"Let It Show"** Have your students name good ways to express feelings. (e.g. talking to family and friends, listening to music that fits your mood, drawing or painting pictures, singing songs, writing stories, doing a good deed, etc.) Have them draw one that they really like.

Play

- ☐ **"Musical Moods"** Play different kinds of music for your students. Afterward, ask:
    - How did the music make you feel?
    - Did the music remind you of any colors?
    - Are there any times when you don't like listening to music?
    - When is it good to listen to quiet music?
    - Do you think music is a good way to relax if you're feeling upset?
- ☐ **"Worry Monster Wipeout!"** Sometimes it is faster to solve problems faster as a team. Ask one student to describe a problem and suggest his two best solutions. Then, ask the class to suggest other solutions to make the worry go away. (e.g. **Had a fight with little sister over toys: share toy next time, remember when you were her age, etc.**) See how many more ideas the class can think of. Repeat the exercise with other problems. Count one point for each solution. See if your class can get more points (i.e. more good solutions) for each consecutive problem.
- ☐ **"Guess That Feeling!"** Have groups of students role play the situations below. Ask the rest of the class how <u>each</u> person would feel in that situation. Discuss how to get help in a dangerous situation.
    - A child loses a favorite toy and his or her mother tries to help.
    - Two children get lost in a big store.
    - A child's friend pushes him or her off a swing.
    - Two children ask a third child to smoke a cigarette.
    - Two children are picking on another student who wears glasses.
    - The principal makes a nice comment about a student's art project.
    - Two students are visiting a friend in the hospital to cheer him or her up.
- ☐ **"Musical Feelings"** Arrange student chairs in a circle. Tape a "feeling" label on each chair (e.g. **happy, sad, etc.**). Play music and have the students march around the chairs. When the music stops, have children sit in the chair closest to them. Ask for volunteers to tell about a time when they felt the feeling shown on their chair's label.
- ☐ **"How many feelings a day?"** Explain that it's normal to have many different feelings in just one day. Ask students for a feeling they experienced that day and why. List all the feelings on the chalkboard. If students slow down, ask if anyone felt (e.g. **happy, sad, etc.**) and why. If no one felt a particular emotion that day, ask students to tell about another time when they had that feeling.
- ☐ **"How Do We Feel?"** Divide your students into small groups. Secretly assign each group a different feeling to act out. Have the other groups try to guess the feeling. The group that answers first gets to go next.
- ☐ **"If You're Happy and You Know It"** Have your students sing the song:

    "If you're happy and you know it, clap your hands."

    Have students create other verses like:

    "If you're sad and you know it, talk it out."

    "If you're angry and you know it, stomp the floor."

PJ's Big Mix Up

Sometimes we feel frustrated or angry or confused. Then we might feel **jumbled like a puzzle** that's all apart. PJ feels that way right now. You can help PJ get back together.

First, cut out PJ's pieces. Second, put them together properly to read PJ's message. Third, paste your pieces onto a clean sheet of paper and color. When you finish, you'll see that PJ has great ideas on how to help you feel better if you ever feel jumbled.

What do you do when you feel jumbled? _____

_____

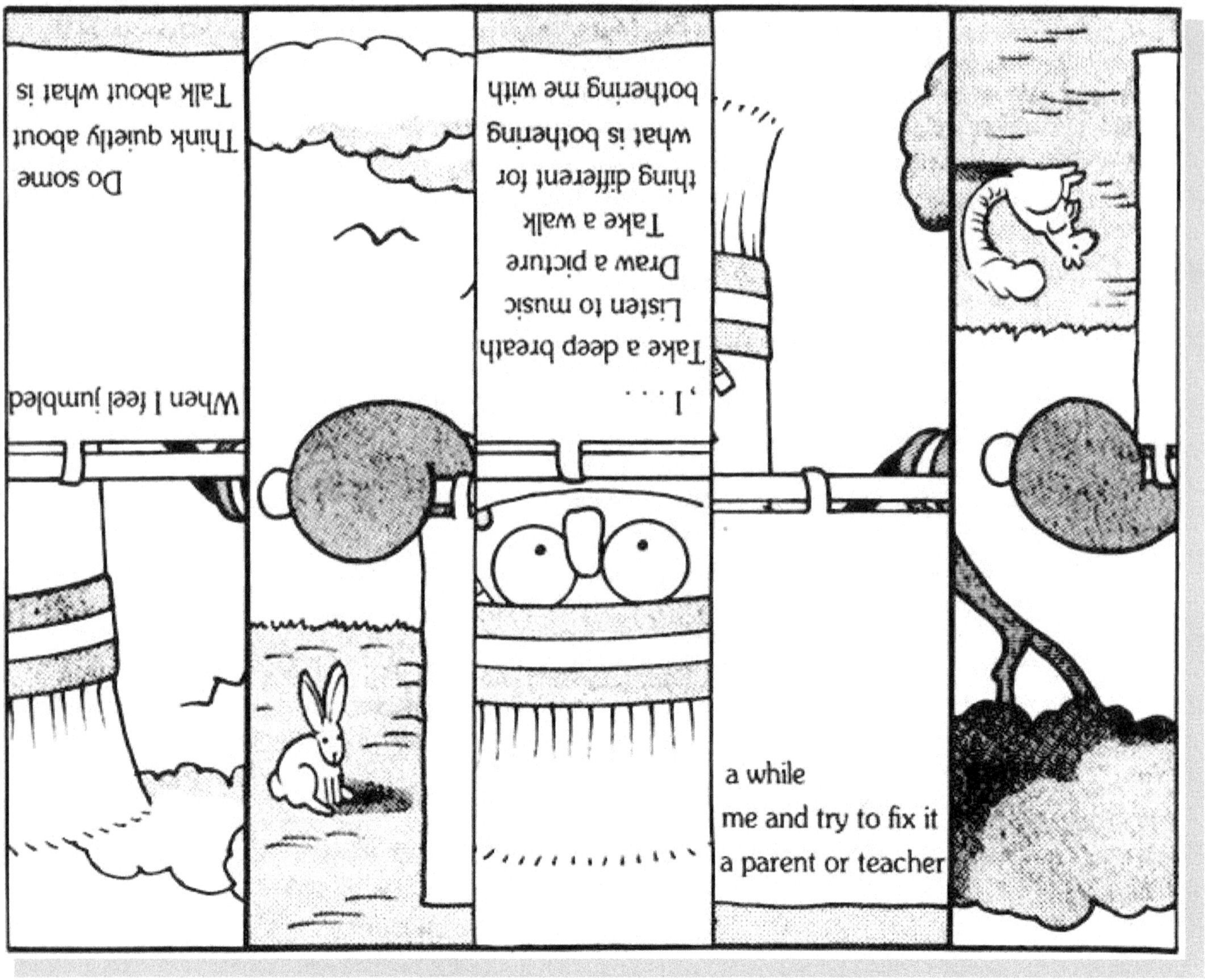

Name _____ Date _____

PARENT'S INITIALS

© Copyright 2008 RoboMedia, Inc. – www.LifeSkills4Kids.com

Storyteller

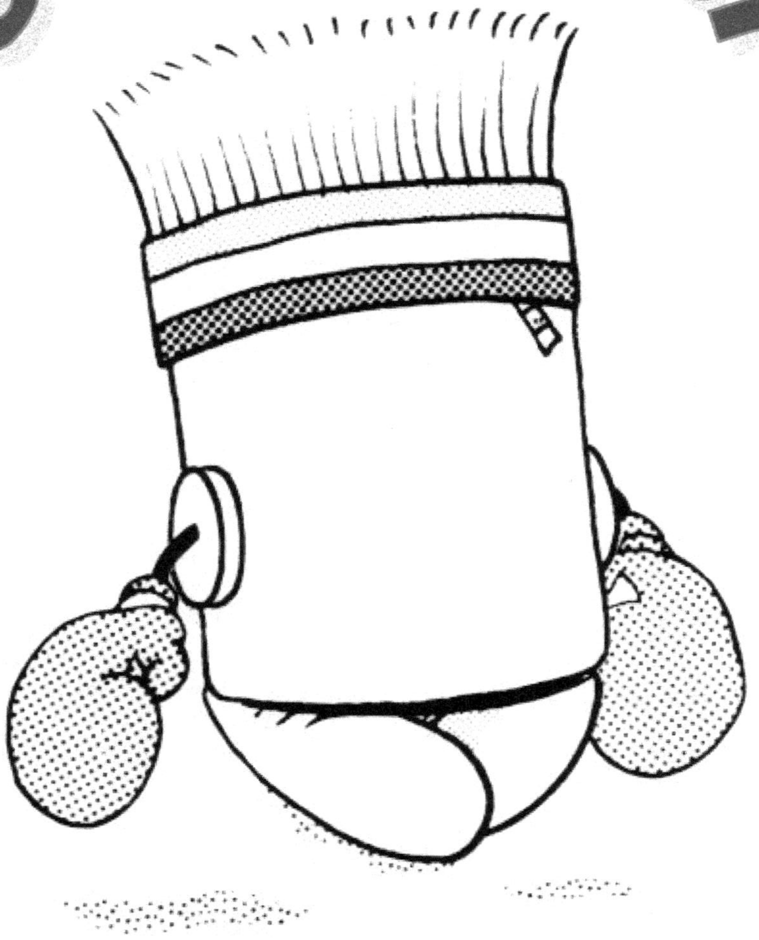

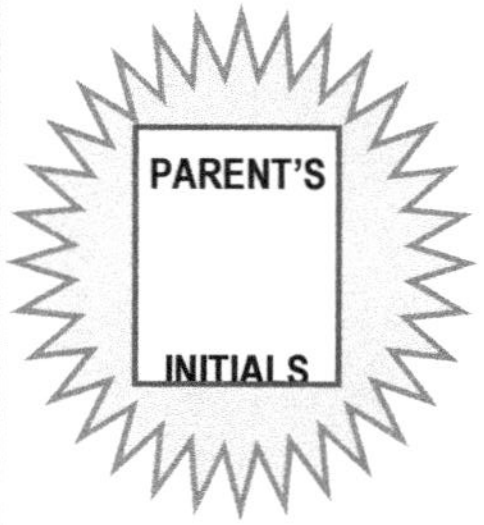

Cut out the faces at the bottom of the page.

Then, sit with a parent and tell a story that gives PJ each of the different feelings. Put the right face on PJ while you are telling the story.

When you are done, pick your favorite story. Glue down the face that goes with that story and color in your worksheet. Bring your worksheet back to class to compare stories with your classmates.

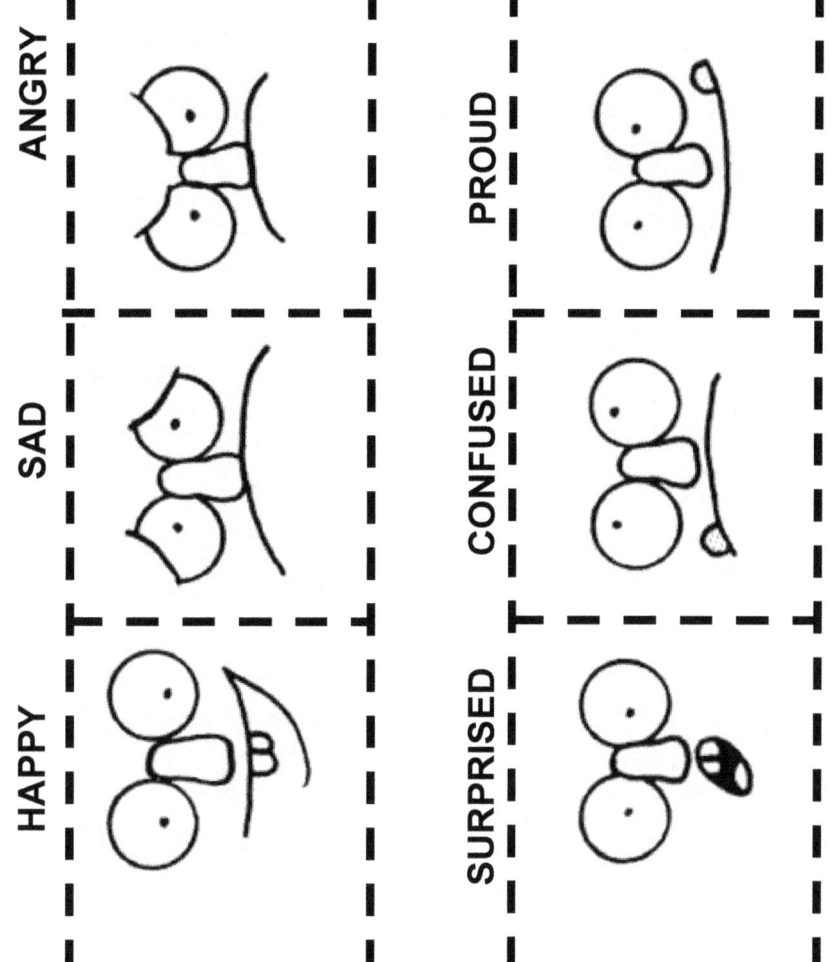

| HAPPY | SAD | ANGRY |
| SURPRISED | CONFUSED | PROUD |

Name _____ Date _____

PARENT'S INITIALS

© Copyright 2008 RoboMedia, Inc. – www.LifeSkills4Kids.com

Self Awareness

3. I take care of my body because it's the most valuable thing I will ever own.

Lesson Notes: In schools, a sophisticated robot teacher can introduce all the learning objectives to students with a live assembly presentation. The program begins by emphasizing how extraordinary the human body is with concrete examples children understand. **The robot teaches children that he isn't the "Million Dollar Machine" that the program is named for; they are!** This lesson helps children understand that their bodies are unique, priceless and irreplaceable. The activities also identify nutrition, rest, exercise and personal hygiene as specific methods of promoting good health.

Talk

- ☐ Why do these lessons call the human body the *Million Dollar Machine*?
- ☐ Do other machines grow and get smarter all the time? How do they change?
- ☐ Why isn't an expensive racing car worth more than your body?
- ☐ Is your body really worth a million dollars? Is it worth more? Why?
- ☐ Why is it so important to take care of your body?
- ☐ Can you ever get a new body?
- ☐ How does food help your *Million Dollar Machine*?
- ☐ Are some foods healthier than others?
- ☐ What can happen if we eat the wrong kinds of foods?
- ☐ Is it possible to eat too much good food?
- ☐ Which is better for your body: rest or exercise?
- ☐ Why is rest and exercise both important?
- ☐ Can you really learn to do anything with your *Million Dollar Machine*?
- ☐ Can your *Million Dollar Machine* really take you anywhere in the world?
- ☐ What can you do to keep your Million Dollar Machine healthy?
- ☐ How does taking care of your Million Dollar Machine help the people around you, too?

Make

- ☐ **"Super Humans"** Have your students name things they can do that a robot can't do.
  (e.g. climb a tree, eat a pizza, go swimming, grow, go up steps, get married, etc.)
  Make a list on the chalkboard. Have each student draw one activity.

- ☐ **"Body Shop"** Robots and other machines can't fix themselves. Your body can fix many of its problems. Ask children to draw ways that their bodies fix themselves.
  (e.g. heals scratches, burns, bruises, broken bones, hair and nails grow, etc.)

- ☐ **"Dear Robot"** Write a letter to the robot teacher about how and why you **"Keep a Clean Machine!"** (This activity is most relevant for children experiencing the live Million Dollar Machine assembly program.)

Self Awareness

- ☐ **"Babysitter"** Have each student draw a baby and some things a baby needs. **(e.g. milk, food, clothes, warm place to sleep, people to care for them, toys, etc.)** Ask children which things they still need. Do adults need them, too? Explain that, as we grow, we get better at getting these things for ourselves and sharing them with other people.

- ☐ **"Body Guard"** It's everyone's job to protect his or her own *Million Dollar Machine*. Ask students to name things they need to protect their bodies from and *how* they protect themselves. **(e.g. alcoholic drinks, tobacco products, drugs, electricity, household chemicals, car accidents, fire, bicycle accidents, guns, etc.)** List the items on the chalkboard, then have students **(or groups)** make up a poster with safety tips about each risk. Have students describe the posters' content to the class when complete.

- ☐ **"Staying In Shape!"** Make a bulletin board with a life sized shape of the human body. Have students look through old magazines and cut out pictures of many different foods and activities. Paste pictures of healthy things inside the outline of the body. Paste pictures of unhealthy things outside the outline of the body.

- ☐ **"Keep a Clean Machine"** Ask your students to name some things they do to stay healthy. **(e.g. eat good foods, exercise, rest, get regular medical and dental checkups, immunizations, wear clean clothes, personal hygiene, etc.)** Have them make posters or a class display showing these concepts.

- ☐ **"Menu Maker"** Have your children draw:
    - nutritious meals for breakfast, lunch, snacks and supper
    - their favorite meal
    - healthy things to drink, etc.

- ☐ **"Healthy Habits"** Have your students name things they do each day to take care of themselves. List them on the chalkboard. **(e.g. eat the right foods, bathe, talk to parents, dress neatly, brush teeth, look for traffic, read, exercise, get enough sleep, wear a seatbelt, etc.)** Then, assign each student a habit to draw. Have students describe their pictures and the importance of each habit.

Play

- ☐ **"Million Dollar Mimes"** Divide your students into small groups. Secretly assign each group a "Healthy Habit" to act out. Have the other groups try to guess the activity. The group that answers first gets to go next.

- ☐ **"Million Dollar Machine Mechanics"** Divide your students into groups. Have each group put on a skits in which they "fix" a problem someone is having with their *Million Dollar Machine*. **(e.g. someone is feeling tired in school so the mechanics make sure the person gets more sleep, eating right and exercising; someone has a cold so the mechanics tell the person to get lots of rest, drink plenty of liquids and see a doctor, etc.)**

- ☐ **"Have a Heart"** Invite the school nurse to measure your students' heart-rates before and after playing an active game. Discuss why the heart works harder when we play. Explain why aerobic exercise (see Wikipedia article) that raises the heart-rate is good for the whole body. It helps our muscle tone, our appearance, our appetite and how well we rest at night. It also helps us to relax and learn more. Have children draw their favorite way to get exercise.

Make a Healthy Meal

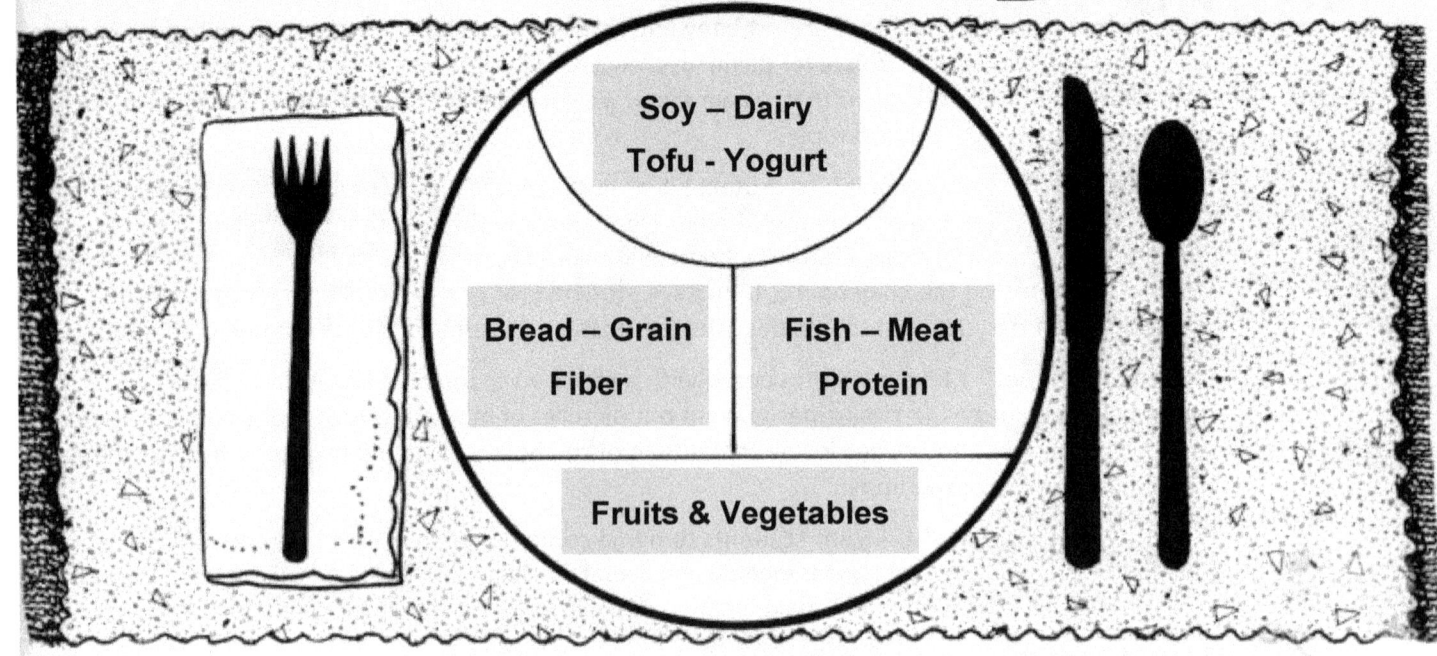

Good food helps your Million Dollar Machine to grow up healthy. The pictures below show some yummy foods. Cut out the food pieces and make healthy meals on the plate. **IDEA: Draw your favorite foods on the back of some pieces!** How many different meals can you make? Glue your **favorite** meal onto the plate and bring back to class to discuss.

Name _____ Date_____

PARENT'S INITIALS

© Copyright 2008 RoboMedia, Inc. – www.LifeSkills4Kids.com

Self Awareness

4. I'll grow up to be my best if I take care of my body.

Lesson Notes: These activities inspire children to set personal goals and stay in school. Educational and behavioral research shows that children as young as 5 years old can adequately conceptualize their future as elementary and junior high school students. Based on these research implications, this lesson emphasizes <u>goal setting</u> and accomplishing future goals. The exercises develop children's ability to control their bodies, feelings and destinies while developing cognitive reasoning skills children need for long-term future orientation.

Talk

- ☐ What is a goal? Why are goals important in life?
- ☐ How long can it take to achieve a goal?
- ☐ Was every **(teacher, athlete, astronaut, scientist, artist, hero, etc.)** your age once?
- ☐ Why is this important to know?
  (e.g. They created their future and achieved their dream. You can, too.)
- ☐ What is a recent goal you have achieved? How long did it take? How did you do it?
- ☐ Who has a goal right now? How long will it take to achieve?
- ☐ How do you get better at something you want to learn to do?
- ☐ How does it feel when you've improved at a game or school subject?
- ☐ Have you ever won a prize for something you've done? How did that feel?
- ☐ What would you like to do when you grow up?
- ☐ Why did you choose that job?
- ☐ Is there anything you can do now to help you reach that goal?
- ☐ Why do we go to school?
- ☐ When do people stop learning?

Make

- ☐ **"I did it!"** Have your students draw pictures of a goal they achieved.
  (e.g. learning to ride a bike, swimming, tying their shoes, reading a book, etc.)
- ☐ **"Certificate of Achievement"** Have children choose an accomplishment they are proud of. Then, have them create certificates for themselves commemorating the occasion. **(e.g. playing a musical instrument, a good grade, completing an art project, learning to ride a bike, etc.)** Hold a class ceremony in which you present each certificate back to the student and ask questions about the accomplishment. **(e.g. How long did it take you? Who helped you learn to do this? What is the next goal you want to achieve? etc.)**
- ☐ **"Goal Getter"** As a class, have your students create an "experience story" or "class story book" about a child who wants to achieve a goal. All of the students should contribute ideas about accomplishing the goal and draw the steps that lead to accomplishment.

# Self Awareness

- ☐ **"My Free Time"** Have students draw a picture of something they like to do in their free time.
- ☐ **"My Next Accomplishment!"** Have students draw a picture of something they want to learn to do next. Have children discuss their goal and how they will achieve it with the class.
- ☐ **"Sweet Dreams"** Have students draw themselves in bed dreaming, with a large bubble over their heads depicting the scene of their dream.
- ☐ **"When I'm Bigger"** Have your students draw a picture of themselves when they are older. **(e.g. 2 years older, 4 years older, 10 years older, etc.)** The pictures should show increased skills as well as maturity and increased size.
- ☐ **"I'll Be A..."** Have students draw what they would like to be when they grow up. This can also be done as a collage with pictures, magazine clippings or art from the Internet.
- ☐ **"Successful People"** Have your students make a class bulletin board with this title. Have them find or draw pictures of individuals (children and adults) who have achieved a major goal in life.
- ☐ **"More Than Money"** Explain that being a success in life doesn't just mean making money. Have your students find or draw pictures showing people enjoying the non-material rewards of success. **(e.g. helping people, respect, family life, happiness, health, learning, travel, etc.)**

Play

- ☐ **"When you were little..."** Have your children close their eyes and remember what it was like to be a baby. Then, ask them to think of things that they couldn't do as babies but are very simple to do now. **(e.g. tie shoelaces, write name, eat with utensils, count, tell time, recite the alphabet, read, go to school, catch a ball, etc.)** Children can take turns showing the class how they did those things as babies and how they do them now. Ask students to talk about some of the people who taught them how to do these things.
- ☐ **"Goal of the week!"** Each week, set a weekly "goal" for the class and ask every student to try to do the goal at least once a day. **(e.g. Give another classmate a compliment. Say "Please" and "Thank-you." Help a classmate. Introduce yourself to a schoolmate you don't know. Help with a chore at home. Pick up some litter and put it in the trash. Etc.)** At the end of the week, ask students for examples of how they met their goal. Ask older students to keep a daily diary of what they did or create a poster and add stars when children tell their goal stories.
- ☐ **"How To?"** Have each student find a "how to" book about something that interests them. Have them learn a skill or fact from the book and share it with the class.
- ☐ **"My Hobby"** Have each student describe or demonstrate to the class a hobby, skill or interest they enjoy. **(e.g. show shell collection, read a poem, play a song, etc.)**
- ☐ **"If at first you don't succeed, try, try again!"** Have your students memorize this phrase. Explain that we all have successes **(things we can do)** and failures **(things we need to try again)**. Talk about how it takes both success and failure to learn and grow. Have students volunteer to describe one success and one thing they want to try again.

CAN DO!

Practice Makes Perfect

Name_____ Date_____

No one is good at *everything*, but everyone is good at *something*. With practice, you can get better at *anything*! Which things are you already good at? Which ones would you like to do better? Check off (✓) your answers.

	I do this well	I want to learn to do this better
Fix a sandwich	_____	_____
Work a computer	_____	_____
Ride a bike	_____	_____
Telephone my house	_____	_____
Count money	_____	_____
Tell time	_____	_____
Write a letter	_____	_____
Make my bed	_____	_____
Read a book	_____	_____

What are some other things you want to learn to do?

_____

_____

_____

PARENT'S INITIALS

© Copyright 2008 RoboMedia, Inc., - www.LifeSkills4Kids.com

"I can be ANYTHING"

When you grow up, you can learn to do anything if you **"Keep a Clean Machine!"**

LAWYER   SENATOR   FIREFIGHTER   PILOT   ACTRESS   DENTIST   VETERINARIAN   JUDGE   CARPENTER   REPORTER

SOCCER PLAYER   POLICE CHIEF   ACTOR   COMPUTER PROGRAMMER

NURSE   ARTIST

Draw what *you* would like to be.

PARENT'S INITIALS

Name _____ Date _____

© Copyright 2008 RoboMedia, Inc. – www.LifeSkills4Kids.com

# Interpersonal Skills

5. Everyone I meet is special.

Lesson Notes: These interactive activities help children understand friendship components that form lasting relationships while practicing courtesy skills. Putting children on the giving and receiving end of good manners improves civility, empathy and social skills to help all classroom activities flow more smoothly. The lessons also examine naturally occurring differences in your community. Depending on your children, neighborhood and school, you may wish to give added attention to <u>ethnicity</u> and racial sensitivity, <u>disability</u> and people with handicaps, people with cultural differences, speak another language or have or any other issues you feel are especially pertinent (<u>cultural competence</u> on Wikipedia).

Talk

- ☐ What are some things that everyone has in common?
  (e.g. all live on Earth, breathe air, need food and water, etc.)
- ☐ What are some things we might have in common with others?
  (e.g. country, school, town, teachers, likes, dislikes, etc.)
- ☐ What are some physical things that make a person unique?
  (e.g. eye color, hair color, sex, ethnic background, height, names, etc.)
- ☐ What are some qualities that make a person unique?
  (e.g. religion, intelligence, compassion, hobbies, skills, etc.)
- ☐ What would the world be like if everyone was the same age?
- ☐ What would the world be like if everyone looked alike?
- ☐ What activities would be difficult if we couldn't tell each other apart?
- ☐ Why are differences a good thing?
- ☐ Are other people's strengths and weaknesses different from our own?
- ☐ Do adults have weaknesses, too? **(e.g. parent raises voice, teacher forgets, etc.)**
- ☐ Is a weakness a good reason to dislike someone?
- ☐ How can you help a person improve a weakness?
  (e.g. be understanding, share your knowledge with them, don't make fun of them, etc.)
- ☐ Can we improve all weaknesses?

Make

- ☐ **"My School Team"** Have your students draw self-portraits and cut them out. Make a wall display of the "class team" pictures using different motifs. **(e.g. on a school bus, in bleachers, as an orchestra, etc.)**
- ☐ **"Heart to Heart"** Distribute multi-colored construction paper. Ask students to cut out small hearts for each of their classmates, write their own name or initials on each heart and give a "signature heart" to each classmate. Have children paste their heart collections on a large piece of paper, forming any shape they please. Point out how each heart is important in each collection and how we are all necessary to make the class a whole.
- ☐ **"Everyone's a Teacher"** Everyone has strengths and weaknesses. A strength is something you do well. A weakness is something you don't do well. You're a "teacher" whenever you help someone else improve a weakness by sharing your strength. Ask your students for examples of things they have taught to others. **(e.g. reading, playing a game, riding a bike, using a computer, etc.)** Have them draw themselves teaching something to a friend.

Interpersonal Skills

Play

- ☐ **"Meet and Greet"** Show your children how to introduce themselves to others. Then, get together with another class for a meet and greet session. Encourage students to exchange information about their favorite hobbies, TV shows, etc. After the session, ask each student to tell the class about one new friend that they met.

- ☐ **"Talent Scout"** Pair students and give them a few minutes to learn about each other's special qualities. Each should pick one of their partner's special qualities and draw a picture of their partner showing that quality. **(e.g. has a big sheepdog, came from another country, speaks a different language, knows how to sew, etc.)**

- ☐ **"Guess My Friend"** Assign each child a "mystery friend" in the class. Have the children think of **three positive traits** and **three physical features** their mystery friend has. These must be **positive** qualities. Have each child describe their "mystery friend" to the class point by point. The first to answer correctly gets to be the next to describe their "mystery friend".

- ☐ **"Everybody's Special"** Explain that each of us has special qualities. No one is exactly like any other person although we have many things in common. Demonstrate this point by giving students instructions to follow, such as:
    - All girls with (black, brown, braided, etc.) hair, raise your hand.
    - Everyone who likes (pizza, salads, yogurt, etc.) stand up.
    - Everyone wearing (a watch, sneakers, etc.) stomp your feet.
    - Everyone who has a (cat, dog, parrot, etc.) imitate your pet's voice.

- ☐ **"Who Are We?"** Have children name different types of people they know. **(e.g. doctor, bus driver, teacher, etc.)** Define the student's relationship with each person and list the pairs on the chalkboard. **(e.g. doctor & patient, bus driver & passenger, teacher & student, parent & child, team member & team member, neighbor & neighbor, classmate & classmate, etc.)**

    Have 2 students come to the front of the class and secretly select one of the relationships from the chalkboard. Then, they role play the relationship while the rest of the students try to guess which one it is. The first person to guess correctly gets to pick a partner and role play another relationship. During the exercise, talk about similarities and differences between people. Look at special skills that make people unique. Establish that we treat everyone with respect, no matter what job they do.

- ☐ **"Lots In Common!"** Have children sit in a circle. How many features can students name that everyone shares? **(e.g. two eyes, two ears, two legs, two arms, wearing shoes, one head, etc.)** Explain that, despite these similarities, we're all different. Next, ask children to name three things about themselves that are different from everyone else.

- ☐ **"Inner Circle"** Take your class outside and have them stand in a circle while you stand in the middle. Explain that you will select a student, say a special quality they have and invite them into the "inner circle." **(e.g. "Sharon, you are special because you help your friends. Join me in the inner circle!")** As they come into the middle, you clap your hands to welcome them. Then, the newest student in the circle repeats the process with a classmate. As more students enter the circle the applause for the remaining students will get louder. The last student joining gets the best welcome of all.

Ace Reporter!

Name _____   Date _____

As an Ace Reporter, you'll learn interesting things about people. Your teacher will pair you up with an interview partner. Take turns interviewing each other. When you are done, compare notes with other reporters in your class.

1. What is your full name? _____

2. How long have you lived here? _____

3. Did you live anywhere else before? _____

4. Do you have brothers or sisters? _____

5. What are their names and ages? _____

6. Do you have any pets? _____

7. What's your favorite color? _____

8. What's your favorite food? _____

9. What's your favorite hobby? _____

10. What's your favorite book? _____

11. What's your favorite school subject? _____

12. What do you want to be when you grow up?
    _____
    _____

PARENT'S INITIALS

© Copyright 2008 RoboMedia, Inc. – www.LifeSkills4Kids.com

Special People - Special Qualities

When you do something well and someone notices, how do you feel?

It feels great when other people notice what you can do!

Everyone is special. Everyone has special qualities. A teacher is loving and patient. A fire fighter is brave to go into a burning building to save a child. A singer has a pretty voice. A friend is generous to share toys with you.

Below are pictures of people you might know. They all have their own special qualities. Write down one special quality under each drawing. The next time you see these people, tell them what makes them special to you. You will make them feel really good.

Your friend's special quality: _____

Your doctor's special quality: _____

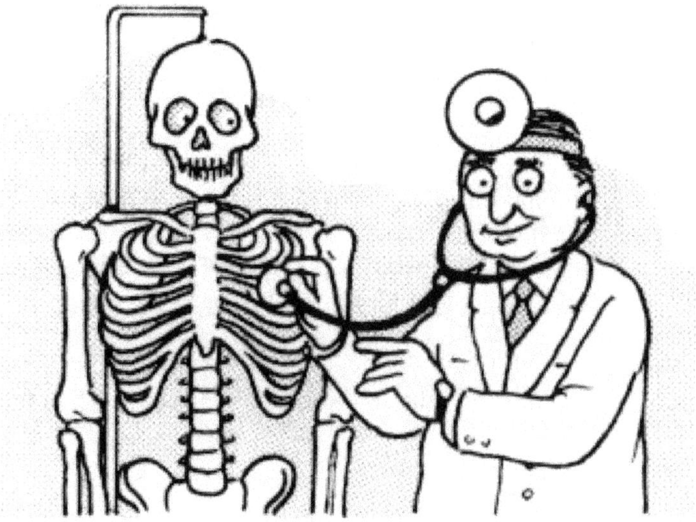

Your teacher's special quality: _____

Your parent's special quality: _____

Name _____ Date _____

PARENT'S INITIALS

© Copyright 2008 RoboMedia, Inc – www.LifeSkills4Kids.com

Interpersonal Skills

6. I respect other people.

Lesson Notes: These activities build on the interpersonal skills introduced in Lesson 5. Many exercises give your children the opportunity to practice courtesy when dealing with others. Again, these lessons encourage children to be empathetic by putting them on the giving and receiving end of good manners. Focusing on increased civility will help all your classroom activities flow more smoothly and prepare children for future teamwork activities.

Talk

- ☐ Why should we be nice to other people?
- ☐ Should we be nice to people who are very different from us? Why?
- ☐ What does "**respect**" mean?
- ☐ Why should we respect the feelings and property of others?
- ☐ Why should we be polite to others?
- ☐ The "Golden Rule" means "Treat others as you would like to be treated." Why is the Golden Rule a good idea? (Read about the global appeal of the "ethic of reciprocity" on Wikipedia)
- ☐ How do you feel if someone is nice **(nasty)** to you?
- ☐ What happens when people are not nice to each other: among your friends? In your family? In the world?
- ☐ How does it feel to be left out of a group activity?
- ☐ What is embarrassment? Jealousy? Anger?
- ☐ What might make us feel these things? Are they normal feelings?
- ☐ What can you do if someone makes you feel **(embarrassed, jealous, angry)**?

Make

- ☐ **"Give a Smile"** Have children make greeting cards for residents of a local nursing home, or for patients at a hospital. Arrange to deliver the cards and talk with your students about how it feels to make other people happy.
- ☐ **"Please and Thank You"** Have your students draw "Please" and "Thank You" signs. Then, read a story, or describe a scene where these words should be used. Have the children hold up their signs and call out the words in unison.
- ☐ **"Pleasing Others"** Have children draw pictures of an activity they do because it is important to someone else. **(e.g. doing chores around the house, getting dressed up for a special occasion, not talking in church, washing the dishes, visiting a relative you don't really like, etc.)** Have each child tell the class why they are happy to do their activity and who enjoys it.
- ☐ **"Thank a Friend"** Have each student make a Thank You card for someone in their family who did something nice for them. Have them give their card to the person and relate the recipient's reaction to the class.
- ☐ **"Manners are in the Bag"** Divide your students into small groups to make lunch-bag puppets. Provide each group with only one pair of scissors, one marker, one spool of yarn and glue. Explain to the children that they should say "please" and "thank you" when they share these items.

Interpersonal Skills

- ☐ **"R E S P E C T"** Have children make a bulletin board with this title. Add drawings or cutout pictures of people showing kindness or good manners. Have children label each picture, for example: "Taking Turns", "Sharing", "Being Helpful", etc.
- ☐ **"Feelings are Fragile"** Ask your students for ideas on how to express negative feelings without hurting someone else. **(e.g. leaving situation, changing subject or activity, talking to adult about problem, etc.)** Make a class poster illustrating some of these ideas.

Play

- ☐ **"Courtesy Circle"** Seat your class in a circle. Start by complimenting a child: "Lisa, I really like your shoes." She says, "Thank you", then compliments the person to her right, and so on. Use the circle to practice other polite phrases, too. (e.g. Pass an object saying "please" and "thank you." "Excuse me, do you know what time it is?" "My name is _____. What's your name?" Etc.)
- ☐ **"Heart of Gold"** Have your students discuss how they show kindness to others. Make a list on the chalkboard. **(e.g. helping a friend who fell, helping the teacher erase the chalkboard, telling someone they are nice, holding a door for someone, giving someone directions, etc.)** Divide students into groups and have them perform skits showing nice things they do for people. Repeat the activity showing how other people show kindness to your students.
- ☐ **"I'd Feel…"** Write down a series of situations on 3 X 5 cards (examples below). Have students pick a card and tell the class how that situation would make him or her feel. Invite other students to comment. Ask for volunteers to relate a similar experience.
  - If my friend hit me, I'd feel…
  - If my friend asked to share my book, I'd feel…
  - If my friend asked me over for dinner, I'd feel…
  - If my friend offered me medicine, I'd feel…
  - If my friend took me to the movies, I'd feel…
  - If my friend called me bad names, I'd feel…
  - If my friend stole something from me, I'd feel…
  - If my friend said nice things to me, I'd feel…
  - If my friend taught me a game, I'd feel…
  - If my friend asked me to do something bad I'd feel.
- ☐ **"Pretend it's You"** Explain to your students that we cannot always say or do what we want. If your comment or action might hurt someone's feelings, you shouldn't do it. Instead, think of something positive to do. Come up with a series of role plays involving awkward situations. Have your students use funny clothes and props to make the activity more fun. **(e.g. Your Aunt Agnes is wearing a really funny hat and asks you if you like it. You could say "It's very different." or "It matches your outfit." or "It's very colorful." Etc.)**

  Other situations might be: **(visiting a friend for dinner and not liking the food; being disappointed by a gift; a friend asks if you like him better than someone else; a visiting relative asks to change the TV channel during your favorite show; a friend asks if you like her drawing and you don't know what it is; Etc.)**
- ☐ **"Share and Share Alike"** Ask your students to bring in toys, games, books, etc. to share with the class. Divide your class into small groups to share the objects among themselves. Point out that everyone should have an opportunity to play with or look at each item. After a set period of time, groups can exchange objects.
- ☐ **"Sssshhhhh"** Explain to your students that we behave differently in different settings. Ask for examples of places we need to be quiet **(e.g. classroom, restaurants, library, church, hospital, theater, etc.)** and for places that we can be noisy **(e.g. swimming pool, amusement park, playground, beach, parties, etc.).** Discuss why we need to change our behavior in different places. Have children do skits showing correct and incorrect behavior for some of the locations.

In NEED of Good DEEDS

Do *you* like it when people are nice to you? Other people like it when you are nice to them, too! Every day, you work, play and study with other people. Some are friends. Some are family. Some are people you don't even know.

The rule to remember is to treat everyone the way *you* like to be treated. Doing good deeds for other people is a great way to show that you are a nice person.

Put a check mark (✓) next to each Good Deed you do for other people this week. Show your parents when you are done. Then, bring your worksheet back to school to share Good Deed stories with classmates.

Share something _____

Open a door for someone _____

Take turns playing with a toy _____

Pick up some trash _____

Help a classmate with a lesson _____

Give someone a compliment _____

Help a young child _____

Help someone with a chore _____

Help someone carry something _____

Pick up something dropped _____

Help with a job at home _____

Name _____ Date _____

PARENT'S INITIALS

© Copyright 2008 RoboMedia, Inc. – www.LifeSkills4Kids.com

How would YOU feel?

Everyone has different feelings. Sometimes you feel sad and sometimes you feel happy. Other people have the same feelings. You should think about how other people feel when things happen to them.

The pictures show kids playing. Some kids are playing nice. Some are not playing nice. Talk with your parents and friends about how you think the different kids feel.

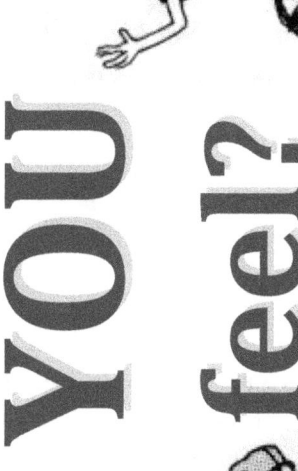

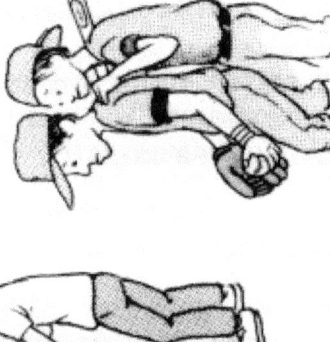

➤ Who is feeling **lonely**? Why?
➤ Who is feeling **proud**? Why?
➤ Who is feeling **happy**? Why?
➤ Who is feeling **sad**? Why?

➤ Who is **sharing** with a friend?
   How will that make the friend feel?
➤ Who is being **mean**?
   How will that make the other person feel?

Name _____ Date _____

PARENT'S INITIALS

© Copyright 2008 RoboMedia, Inc. - www.LifeSkills4Kids.com

Interpersonal Skills

7. I use teamwork when I work and play with other people.

Lesson Notes: Within the context of social settings with other children, these activities teach individual responsibility, self-discipline and the ability to differentiate between right and wrong behavior. Children exhibiting these qualities are less likely to try drugs or other risky behaviors than those who do not value responsibility and self-discipline.

Talk
- ☐ What is "**team spirit**"?
- ☐ What is "**cooperation**"?
- ☐ Why is it important to share?
- ☐ What does it feel like to belong to a team, or a close group of friends?
- ☐ What are some groups that you belong to?
  (e.g. family, class, church groups, scouting, hobby groups, musical groups, clubs, etc.)
- ☐ Why do you enjoy activities with those groups?
- ☐ In a game like basketball or soccer, why is it sometimes better to pass the ball instead of going for the shot?
- ☐ Is it quicker to do things working alone or working as a team?
- ☐ Why are rules necessary when playing on a team?
- ☐ What are some rules you follow at home?
- ☐ What are some rules you follow in school?
- ☐ Who is more important, the teacher or the students?
- ☐ Are teachers and students both needed to have a school?

Make
- ☐ **"I Love My Team!"** Make up a sheet with all your student's names in a column on the left. Make copies for each student. Then, have students write a positive comment next to each child's name. Bind the pages together and have students take turns reading the comments.
- ☐ **"My Favorite Team"** Ask your students to draw the team activity that they enjoy most.
- ☐ **"Team Art"** Divide your class into groups to create art posters about a "group" or "team" they might belong to. **(e.g. Americans, elementary students, children, humans, friends, etc.)** Assign a different subject to each group. Assign each student a unique task, drawing tool or scene element to draw. **(e.g. Each student only uses one color. Each student draws a different type of object like plants, objects, animals or people. Each student draws things starting with different letters. Etc.)** Encourage students to help each other with ideas and suggestions.
- ☐ **"Rules Make Things Run at Home"** Have your students give examples of rules they follow at home while you write them on the chalkboard. **(e.g. turn off lights when you leave a room, clean up your own mess, help with the dishes, no fighting, go to bed at a certain time, etc.)** When you have a good list, assign specific rules to groups of students to draw. Hang the drawings together and review them, discussing the importance of each one.
- ☐ **"Rules for Good Citizenship"** Have your students give examples of rules that are important in the community while you write them on the chalkboard. **(e.g. cross streets at corners, obey the crossing guard, don't litter, etc.)** When you have a good list, assign specific rules to groups of students to draw. Hang the drawings together and review them, discussing the importance of each one.

Interpersonal Skills

- **"Class Rules"** Explain that classroom rules help everyone to learn more and to have more fun. Have students name the rules of your classroom while you write them on the chalkboard. (e.g. saying "please" and "thank you," raising your hand to speak, not interrupting others, not cutting in line, sharing classroom equipment, etc.) When you have a good list, assign specific rules to groups of students to draw. Hang the drawings together and review them, discussing the importance of each one.

- **"Good Citizen"** Have your students create a large mural depicting wholesome community activities and acts of good citizenship. Arrange for a local community group (e.g. Chamber of Commerce, PTA, Red Cross, City Hall etc.) to publicly display the mural after its completion. Depending on the group, different health themes could be included in the mural.

Play

- **"Class Story"** Tell your students that they are going to write a story together. Start with a phrase like "Today, I was going to make a new friend. Here's what happened..." Have each child add a sentence to the story. Record the story and make copies for the class.

- **"Go Team, Go!"** Divide your class into groups of 2 to 10 students. Distribute paper and explain that each group must write down all the letters of the alphabet and one word starting with each letter. The group can divide responsibilities as they wish. (e.g. one student may do A-M and another does N-Z, or one student writes all the answers, etc.) Signal the students to start and tell them to stand up when they are done. This activity could also be done counting objects like buttons or beans.

  When all the groups are done, talk about why some teams completed the assignment faster than others. Ask for other examples of how teamwork can affect a project. (e.g. building a house, manufacturing cars, sports team, rescue operation, orchestra, etc.)

- **"Puzzle Relay"** Get some simple jigsaw puzzles. Divide your class into teams of three to five students. Have the teams stand away from the puzzles. To begin, one team member goes up to a puzzle, places a piece, then "tags" the next team member. Repeat this exercise several times, mixing teams and puzzles to give everyone a chance to win.

- **"My Contribution"** Create a list of classroom duties with your students. Write the duties on 3 X 5 cards. Each week, have students select a card to find their special job. (e.g. picking out a story or filmstrip, feeding the classroom pet, picking up classroom trash, cleaning desks, washing the chalkboard, taking attendance, etc.)

- **"Good Citizen Sighted!"** Tell students that people notice when they do good deeds. Cover a small box with contact paper and label it: "Good Citizen Sightings." Put a stack of small pieces of paper next to the box. Ask students to be on the lookout for students doing good deeds. (e.g. good manners, helping others, being friendly, etc.) Once a day, students should take a paper, write down a good deed they saw and who they saw doing it. At the end of the week, read some slips to the class. Children keep the slips that are about themselves.

- **Visitor Idea** - Invite a police officer, fireman, rescue worker or community figure to speak to your class about community rules and safety. Before they arrive, write a list of questions on the chalkboard to get the conversation started. Include a discussion about teamwork in your list of topics. After the visit, have students draw or tell one thing that they learned.

Play by the Rules

We follow lots of different rules everyday. There are rules at home and rules at school. There are rules for using your bike safely and there are rules about being polite to people. You can learn the rules to follow from your parents, teachers and friends.

Following rules is always a big help to everyone. Decide whether the following situations follow the rules or break them. Put a check (✓) on the side you think is right.

Follows the rules   **Breaks the rules**

_____ ******************* **talking during class** ******************* _____
_____ ***************doing your homework with a friend*************** _____
_____ *******************opening a door for someone*************** _____
_____ *********************being late for school********************* _____
_____ ****************helping someone with a problem************** _____
_____ *******************sharing a book with a friend**************** _____
_____ **********************smoking cigarettes*********************** _____
_____ *****************running in the halls at school***************** _____
_____ ************************talking on the bus*********************** _____
_____ **********saying "please" when you want something********** _____
_____ **********taking a toy that doesn't belong to you********** _____
_____ *********************hitting another child********************* _____
_____ ****************throwing trash in the trash can************** _____
_____ ***************calling another person terrible names********* _____

Name_____ Date_____

PARENT'S INITIALS

© Copyright 2008 RoboMedia, Inc., www.LifeSkills4Kids.com

TEAM SPIRIT!

People help other people all the time. Different people help you in different ways. You help other people in many ways too. How many questions can you answer? Fill out this sheet with your parents!

Who wakes you up in the morning? _____

Who fixes your breakfast? _____

Who drives you to and from school? _____

Who makes the lunch you eat at school? _____

Who teaches you to spell? _____

Who do you go to if you don't feel well? _____

Who is in charge of your school? _____

Who helps keep you healthy? _____

Who cuts your hair? _____

Who keeps your neighborhood safe? _____

Who can help you make an emergency phone call? _____

Who are some other people who help you? _____

What are some things you do to help other people?

_____

Name _____

Date _____

© Copyright 2008 RoboMedia, Inc. www.LifeSkills4Kids.com

Interpersonal Skills

8. I am a good friend.

Lesson Notes: These activities help children understand the friendship components that help form lasting relationships. The exercises provide opportunities for your students to interact and learn from each other while practicing courtesy skills. Putting children on the both giving and receiving end of good manners improves civility, empathy and interactive skills that will help all your classroom activities flow more smoothly.

The Wikipedia article on Friendship and www.friendship.com.au are good resources with many links.

Talk

- ☐ What is a friend? See the Wikipedia article on friendship.
- ☐ What are some qualities a friend should have?
  (e.g. kind, generous, a sense of humor, patient, sensitive, dependable, helpful, etc.)
- ☐ How important is it to have friends?
- ☐ Should we be friendly to people who aren't our friends? Why or why not?
- ☐ Does friendship just happen or do you make it happen?
- ☐ How did you meet some of your friends?
- ☐ What are some qualities a friend should have?
  (e.g. kindness, humor, patience, generosity, sensitivity, helpfulness, etc.)
- ☐ How did you meet some of your friends?
- ☐ How are you and your friends alike?
- ☐ How are you and your friends different?
- ☐ How do we show our friends we like them?
  (e.g. talk to them, listen to them, help them, share, play together, etc.)
- ☐ Why is it important to let people know how we feel?
- ☐ Sometimes, should we keep our feelings to ourselves? When?
  (e.g. when it is impolite, might make someone feel bad, when we are angry, etc.)
- ☐ Which are better: older or younger friends? Does age make a big difference?
- ☐ Do friends like to do the same things all the time? If not, why are they still friends?
- ☐ Would a friend ever ask you to do something dangerous?
- ☐ Would a friend ever offer you drugs?

Make

- ☐ **"Be a Friend to Keep a Friend"** If you want to have friends, you have to be a friend. Have your children name some things friends do for each other. **(e.g. talk to each other, listen carefully to each other, help each other, share things, play together, etc.)** Then, ask them to draw something they did with a friend recently.
- ☐ **"Special Greeting"** Have your students think of a special friend. Have them make a greeting card for that person expressing some reasons why they like them. **(e.g. you treat me nice, you share with me, you helped me look for my dog, you walk home from school with me, etc.)** Have students distribute their cards and report the friend's reaction back to the class.

Interpersonal Skills

- ☐ **"Fun With My Friends!"** Have your students make a bulletin board with this title. Have them decorate it with slogans, pictures, drawings, buttons, etc. related to the theme.

- ☐ **"Friendship Recipe"** Divide your class into groups. Have each group develop a "Friendship Recipe" that includes ingredients that are part of a good friendship. Each group should write down their "Friendship Recipe" on a large piece of paper to display to the class. Decorate the recipe with drawings and pictures. Bind the recipe cards together with yarn to make a class recipe book. Swap recipe books with other classes to see what ingredients the students share.

- ☐ **"Friendship Garden"** Have each child bring in a wallet size photo of themselves. Put these in a hat and have each student take a photo. Explain that each student will make a flower using the photo of his or her classmate in the center. Have them cut out petals from multi-colored craft paper and glue them around the face in the photo. Attach wire or pipe cleaners for stems. Create a friendship garden by "planting" all the flowers in a box.

- ☐ **"Express Yourself"** Have each child make an art project for a friend in another class. Have them give the gifts to their friends and report their friend's reactions back to the class.

Play

- ☐ **"Buddy System"** Assign each student a "buddy." Have buddies share activities, duties and assignments during the school day. Buddies are also responsible for making sure their buddy is safe and on time. Switch buddies on a weekly basis.

- ☐ **"Tips for Making Friends"** Ask your students to help you come up with ways to make new friends. Write their ideas on the board. **(e.g. listen to what people have to say, ask people about themselves, join new clubs or activities, introduce yourself, see what you have in common, make a joke, share something, help someone, etc.)** Then, divide students into groups to role play situations showing how to use one of the rules. You may want to type the tips and make a copy of the ideas for each student.

- ☐ **"New Kid on the Block"** Divide your class into small groups. Have each group talk about what it's like to be new to a school or neighborhood. Then, have each group role play a skit where one child is new to the school. Have "new" students demonstrate different ways of making friends to the class. Have "local" students show ways to make new people feel welcome.

- ☐ **"Pooh"** Read a Winnie the Pooh story to your class. With your students discuss how Winnie the Pooh, Christopher Robin, Tiger, Eeyore, Piglet and Owl are friends. Ask for examples of friendly things the characters did for each other. Discuss why the characters like each other and how they play together. This Wikipedia article on Winnie The Pooh will help.

- ☐ **"Open Sesame"** In 2008, Sesame Street has run for 39 seasons, making it one of the longest running shows in TV history. Watch an episode of Sesame Street with your class. Then, ask your students to volunteer to play some of the Sesame Street characters. Have them act out different scenes from the episode, treating each other like Sesame Street characters do. Develop lessons on friendship related to the episode. For example, remind students that everyone is nice to Oscar even though he growls a lot. The Wikipedia article on Sesame Street is a great information source for teachers and parents.

All About Friends

Balloons: Treat Them Nice. / Ask What THEY Want To Do. / Say Please, Thank You. / Help Them. / Be Yourself. / Compliment Them. / Listen To Them. / Share With Them.

Everyone likes to have friends. But friendships don't just happen; you have to **work at them**. How many of PJ's hints about making and keeping friends do you use?

With your parents, fill in the sentences below with words from your Word Bank. Do you do some of these things with your friends?

WORD BANK

| feelings | thank you | invite | please |
| share | help | listen | different |

1. Even if someone looks _____, they can still be my friend.

2. I _____ my toys with my friends.

3. I _____ to a friend who has something to tell me.

4. If my friend had a problem, I try to _____.

5. If I am mean to my friends, it might hurt their _____.

6. I always say "_____" when someone gives me something.

7. Sometimes, I _____ my friends over to my house to play.

8. When I want someone to do something for me I always say "_____."

9. Write down some nice things that you have done for friends:
   _____

PARENT'S INITIALS

Name_____ Date_____

© Copyright 2008 RoboMedia, Inc. – www.LifeSkills4Kids.com

Friends Together

Name _____ Date _____

You and your friends work and play together every day. The pictures show kids doing things you probably do with your friends.

Read the activity list at the bottom with a parent. Point to kids in the pictures doing each activity. When was the last time you did something like that?

v Caring for a hurt friend.
v Taking turns with friends.
v Playing together.
v Teaching a friend.
v Helping a friend play.
v Sharing with a friend.

PARENT'S INITIALS

© Copyright 2008 RoboMedia, Inc. – www.LifeSkills4Kids.com

Interpersonal Skills

9. I'm an important part of my family.

Lesson Notes: These activities help children recognize the importance of their own family, regardless of whether their family conforms to stereotypes or common social norms. It looks at how families vary in size, composition, number of parents and parent surrogates, etc. The exercises demonstrate that your students are already part of "normal families" and that every family is a "typical family" in its own special way. In conducting these activities, avoid indications that one type of family is preferred more or less than another type.

Talk

- ☐ What is a "<u>family</u>"?
- ☐ Are all families the same?
- ☐ What are some things your family gives you?
  (e.g. love, a place to live, protection, nutrition, companionship, etc.)
- ☐ What are some things you give your family?
  (e.g. love, help with chores, pride, companionship, etc.)
- ☐ What are some different types of families?
  (e.g. two parent, just a father, just a mother, mother with step-father, etc.)
- ☐ Who is in your family?
- ☐ How did you become a part of your family?
- ☐ What are some things that can change a family?
  (e.g. birth, illness, adoption, sibling leaving home, having a grandparent move in, having a handicapped or invalid family member move in, parental separation, divorce, remarriage, death, etc.)
- ☐ What are some things that families do together?
- ☐ Is it important to respect the privacy of other family members?
- ☐ Does everyone in a family have responsibilities?
- ☐ What are some responsibilities you have to your family?
  (e.g. keep my room clean, help dry dishes, watch my little brother, rake the yard, etc.)
- ☐ Whose job is it to keep your home safe?
- ☐ Whose job is it to keep your home clean?

Make

- ☐ **"Family Units"** Have your children cut pictures out of magazines to make different family units.
  (e.g. 2 parents, single parent, children living with grandparents, only child, brothers and sisters, etc.)
- ☐ **"Family Portrait"** Have your students draw pictures of their families. Have them label the name and role of each family member. **(e.g. Mom - Mrs. Smith, Dad - Mr. Smith, sister - Sue, Fido - pet, etc.)** Hang the pictures up so that students can see the different types of families their classmates have.
- ☐ **"Our Favorite Room"** Have your students draw a room in their home where their family does things together. When they finish, have them tell the class the kinds of activities they do together in that room.

Interpersonal Skills

- ☐ **"Caring for Each Other"** Ask your students to share ways that they care for members of their families. Have them draw pictures of themselves helping a family member. Then, ask them to draw a picture of a family member helping them.
- ☐ **"Why You're Special"** Have students make greeting cards for each member of their family. Have them say something in the card about why that family member is so special to them.
- ☐ **"Things We Do Together"** Have your students draw an activity they do with their family. **(e.g. having picnics, going to church, eating dinner, shopping, going to the movies, visiting relatives, training pets, etc.)** Then, have them write down some things that they do to help their family prepare for the activity.

Play

- ☐ **"It's My Job"** Have your students take turns miming a helping activity they do around the house. **(e.g. taking out the trash, raking leaves, washing dishes, making a bed, etc.)** Have the other students guess what the activity is. Whoever guesses correctly first gets to go next.
- ☐ **"You Must Have Been a Beautiful Baby!"** Ask students to bring in baby pictures of themselves. Write names on the back and arrange the photos on a bulletin board.
  Invite students to try to guess which baby picture belongs to which student.
- ☐ **"Bringing Up Baby"** Using a doll, have pairs of students, and individual students, pretend to be the adult care-givers in various situations. **(e.g. grandmother is coming to see baby, baby is hungry, baby is sick, etc.)** Discuss how men and women can both care for infants.
- ☐ **"Y.O.M.O."** Divide your class into 4 groups:
    - o **Y**oungest child in family
    - o **O**ldest child in family
    - o **M**iddle child in family
    - o **O**nly child in family

  Have each group meet in a different corner of the classroom. Have them discuss what it is like to be in that group. **(e.g. What's good about it? What's not good about it? Would they rather be in a different group? Why? etc.)** Each group selects a spokesperson to report what they learned together to the class. Conclude the exercise by showing how each child has a special role to play in his/her family.
- ☐ **"If It Weren't for Me!"** Have your students draw pictures of things they do to help their families. Then, have them draw pictures of what might happen if they didn't do their job. **(e.g. take out trash - giant pile of trash builds up, helping with ironing – parent ironing alone late at night, clean up room - can't open door to room, etc.)**

  Discuss with your class how helping out at home is very important to their family. Encourage them to be proud of their contributions.

"Who does it?"

You're an important member of your family team!
Everyone in your home has different responsibilities. When everyone works together, all the jobs get done. Sit with a family member and read the jobs below.

Write down who does each job to the right.
If everyone helps with that job, write "everyone."

Put a star (☆) to the left of all the jobs you help with.

List your family members here:

_____   _____
_____   _____
_____   _____

My Job	Household Job	Who does this job most?
☆	Who keeps your room clean?	I do
___	Who answers the phone?	_____
___	Who turns out the lights?	_____
___	Who takes out the trash?	_____
___	Who cleans the yard?	_____
___	Who feeds the pet(s)?	_____
___	Who makes breakfast?	_____
___	Who goes food shopping?	_____
___	Who cooks dinner?	_____
___	Who washes the dishes?	_____
___	Who helps you study?	_____
___	Who vacuums the house?	_____
___	Who washes the car?	_____
___	Who pays the bills?	_____
___	Who checks the mail?	_____
___	Who does the laundry?	_____

PARENT'S INITIALS

Name _____   Date _____

© 2008 RoboMedia, Inc. – www.LifeSkills4Kids.com

Dear Parent,

Your child is learning the importance of responsibility and helping others.

Will you please think of special jobs he or she can do at home? List the jobs on the left side of this worksheet. Then, have your child draw a star on the line to the right each time a job is done.

Let these jobs be your child's **personal responsibility**. Have your child write their name below and **return this worksheet to class** by _____.

(Name) _____ **has completed these helpful jobs around the house:**

PARENT'S INITIALS

1. _____   ☆ ___ ___ ___ ___ ___

2. _____   ☆ ___ ___ ___ ___ ___

3. _____   ☆ ___ ___ ___ ___ ___

4. _____   ☆ ___ ___ ___ ___ ___

5. _____   ☆ ___ ___ ___ ___ ___

© Copyright 2008 RoboMedia, Inc. – www.LifeSkills4Kids.com

Decision Making

10. I make important decisions for myself every day.

Lesson Notes: Developing self-responsibility is a major goal of this curriculum. These exercises help children recognize <u>decision making</u> opportunities that are part of the normal daily routine, even for the youngest children. The activities demonstrate how your children can make their decisions work for them, by stopping bad habits and evaluating outside influences, such as advertising.

Talk

- ☐ What is a decision?
- ☐ How do your decisions control your *Million Dollar Machine*?
- ☐ What are some things we can't decide for ourselves?
   (e.g. who our parents are, grade on test, what school to go to, what medicine to take, who rides our bus, etc.)
- ☐ What are some things we can decide for ourselves?
   (e.g. our friends, our favorite food, etc.)
- ☐ What kinds of decisions do you make every day?
   (e.g. what to eat for breakfast, what to wear, how hard I study, where to sit on the bus, etc.)
- ☐ What decisions do you make about caring for yourself and your body?
   (e.g. deciding not to smoke, eating the right foods, getting enough rest, not doing dangerous things, etc.)
- ☐ How do you know the difference between right and wrong?
- ☐ If you make a bad decision, can you change your mind?
- ☐ Why should you admit it when you have made a wrong decision?
- ☐ What are bad habits? Can you decide to get rid of a bad habit?
- ☐ How do you decide which products to use?
   (e.g. toy, movie, cereal, game, food, etc.)
- ☐ Do ads try to influence your decisions? How?
- ☐ How do you decide if a product is good or bad?
- ☐ Is everything you see on television or in a magazine true?
- ☐ What are some differences between real life and television?
- ☐ What are some things you see on television that could hurt you in real life?

Make

- ☐ **"Decisions, Decisions!"** Have your students draw pictures of decisions that they make every day.
   (e.g. what to wear, what to eat, what to read, who to play with, etc.)
- ☐ **"Advisors"** Have your students draw a picture of someone who helps them know the difference between right and wrong. **(e.g. parents, teacher, baby sitter, older siblings, etc.)**
- ☐ **"Bashing Bad Habits"** Explain to your students that by making smart decisions, they can get rid of any bad habit. List some bad habits on the chalkboard. **(e.g. interrupting, biting nails, watching too much TV, etc.)** Have students suggest ideas for overcoming them. **(e.g. substitute healthy activity, ask others to look for your bad habit, set a decreasing limit on how many times a day you can do the bad habit, etc.)** Then, have students draw pictures of bad habits and healthy habits to replace them with.
- ☐ **"Warning! Dangerous Products!"** Make a bulletin board with this title. Tell students that some products have warnings right in the ad. **(e.g. tobacco, alcohol, medicines, recreational vehicles, etc.)** Have them cut examples out of magazines. Then, ask your students if they think the warnings are a good idea and why.

Decision Making

- ☐ **"Advertiser for the Day"** As a group activity, have students design ads for healthy products. (e.g. foods, exercise equipment, toys, clothes, museums, books, etc.) Tell them to make the products look attractive and interesting. Have your class discuss and evaluate each ad afterwards. (e.g. Was it eye-catching? Did the ad show people enjoying the product? Was everything said in the ad completely true? Etc.)

Play

- ☐ **"Just In Time!"** Ask children to relate stories about a time they changed their mind and it worked out for the best. (e.g. Wanted a toy - found out it wasn't much fun by playing with one; thought about yelling at someone about a mistake they made - decided not to and found out you actually made the mistake; etc.) After a few stories, divide students into groups to create a skit about a time someone changed their mind and things worked out for the best.

- ☐ **"Good Decisions for Bad Habits"** Divide your students into small groups. Ask each group to decide on a bad habit to role play. (e.g. biting finger nails, watching too much TV, not sharing, drinking too many soft drinks, eating too many sweets, etc.) Explain that people usually don't change their behavior until they realize that bad things happen because of bad habits. Have the groups present their skits to the class, acting out the habit, why it was bad and what they did to stop it.

- ☐ **"Berenstain Bears Too Much TV"** and **"Berenstain Bears Junk Food"** are two stories to read and discuss with your class. Wikipedia has a useful article on the Berenstain series.

- ☐ **"Smart Shopper Sweep"** Have students bring in **empty** product packages to create a classroom collection. Include as many types of consumer products as possible (e.g. foods, medicines, cleaning supplies, tobacco products, alcoholic beverages, soda, etc.). Be sure all containers are washed well. Randomly set containers out on tables around your classroom. Instruct pairs of students to collect as many products as possible from one category in a set time period. (e.g. unhealthy products, healthy products, fruit and vegetable products, grain products, medicines, cleaning products, etc.) Provide baskets for students to make it easy.

- ☐ **"Healthy Choice"** Have each student bring in an empty box of their favorite breakfast cereal. Arrange cereals according to protein, fiber and/or sugar content **(Consumer Reports is a good resource)**. Discuss the benefits of getting enough protein and fiber and not eating too much sugar. Explain that children can use decision-making skills when selecting a cereal. Discuss what kinds of cereal are healthy and which cereal your students will choose to eat in the future.

- ☐ **"Ad Court"** Explain to students that ads on TV, signs and magazines are there because advertisers want their money. Most of the time advertisers offer good products. Sometimes, products are unhealthy or bad. Have students cut out a collection of magazine ads. (e.g. food, medicine, toys, clothing, cigarettes, alcohol, etc.) Hold ads up for everyone to see and have the class vote on whether an item is healthy or unhealthy. Have two students at the chalkboard keep a count of ads in each group.

- ☐ You can also come up with your own categories to inspire discussion. (e.g. Necessities vs. Luxuries, etc.) You could also discuss particular ads in more detail. (e.g. Does the ad tell the whole truth about the product? Could the product hurt your health in any way? Does the ad tell any bad things about the product? Etc.)

- ☐ **"TV Celebrity"** Make a "TV set" out of a cardboard box with aluminum foil and paint. Give each student a chance to perform a live commercial for a product that is healthy for children.

Who's in Charge?

Every day, your parents and teachers help you make decisions.
You make many important decisions for yourself, too!
As you get older and smarter, you will make more decisions for yourself.
On the list below, circle who makes the decision.
More than one person may share some decisions.

Who decides:

My favorite color?	(me)	teacher	parent
When I go to bed?	me	teacher	parent
What I study in school?	me	teacher	parent
What I have for dinner?	me	teacher	parent
What grade I get in spelling?	me	teacher	parent
Who I sit with on the bus?	me	teacher	parent
Who my friends are?	me	teacher	parent
What my favorite game is?	me	teacher	parent
If I should help a friend?	me	teacher	parent
If I go to school?	me	teacher	parent
What medicines I take?	me	teacher	parent
If I'm nice to someone?	me	teacher	parent
Where I sit in class?	me	teacher	parent
What I watch on TV?	me	teacher	parent
How I spend my money?	me	teacher	parent
If I tell the truth?	me	teacher	parent

Name_____ Date_____

PARENT'S INITIALS

© Copyright 2008 RoboMedia, Inc. – www.LifeSkills4Kids.com

Decisions...Decisions!

What is a *decision*? A decision is when there are *different things* you can do and you pick *one* of them. You make lots of decisions every day!

Some decisions are easy; like choosing a book to read. Some decisions are hard; like deciding the best birthday present to get a friend! Here's a list of things you decide for yourself. Write your decisions and why you made each decision.

1. When I got dressed for school, I put on _____.

   I decided to wear that because _____.

2. For breakfast, I had _____.

   I decided to eat that because _____.

3. On my way to school I talked to _____.

   I decided to talk to them because _____.

4. A book I really like is _____.

   I decided to read that book because _____.

5. My favorite game to play is _____.

   I decided to play that game because _____.

6. I share _____ with my friends.

   I decided to share that with my friends because _____.

7. What is a decision you made today? _____.

   Why did you decide to do that? _____.

Name_____ Date_____

PARENT'S INITIALS

© Copyright 2008 RoboMedia, Inc. – www.LifeSkills4Kids.com

Decision Making

11. I know ways to solve many of my own problems.

Lesson Notes: This section gives K-3 children one of the most important tools in this curriculum: **a simplified but effective problem solving model.** Using this system clarifies the steps of problem solving, giving children more confidence in learning to solve their own problems. Many of these activities also develop cooperation and group problem solving strategies. Scientific evaluations of students using the Million Dollar Machine curriculum demonstrated significant improvements in problem solving and decision-making skills.

Talk
- ☐ What is the difference between a decision and a problem?
- ☐ Does everyone have problems to solve?
- ☐ Do problems go away by themselves?
- ☐ What are some problems that can usually be avoided? (e.g. being late, getting burned, etc.)
- ☐ Why do problems confuse us sometimes? (e.g. missing some facts, new problem, etc.)
- ☐ Can you solve every problem? What can you do if you are confused by a problem?
- ☐ How do you solve problems? (see "3 Steps to Solutions" below)
- ☐ How does knowing the difference between right and wrong help you solve problems?
- ☐ What's a "**consequence**"? (the result of an *action*. This is what happens next when you do something.)
- ☐ What are some examples of positive and negative consequences?
(e.g. helped a friend - she smiled and thanked me; broke a school rule - got punished, etc.)

Make
- ☐ **"3 Steps to Solutions"** Explain to your students that there are 3 steps to help them make better decisions: **LIST** all the things you could do! **COMPARE** your choices. Some will have better consequences (results) than others! **CHOOSE** the one that's best! Have each student make a sign showing these 3 steps with an example problem. Hang them in the classroom.
- ☐ **"A Stitch in Time"** Ask your students for decisions they make that *prevent* problems from happening. (e.g. keeping shoes tied, not talking to strangers, looking both ways before crossing street, washing hands before eating, etc.) Have them draw pictures of these situations. Discuss how *preventing a problem* is usually much *easier* than solving a problem that has happened.
- ☐ **"C'est la vie!"** (pronounced 'Say-La-Vee') Tell your children this is a French phrase that means *'That's life!'* French people say this when something happens they can't control. No one can control everything in life. The following stories are very similar but there is one big difference. One child could have avoided the problem but the other child couldn't. See if you can figure out which is which. Work with students to create other short story examples.
    1. Bart made a ramp out of bricks and plywood to ride his bike over. On his first jump, the ramp collapsed. Bart broke his arm.
    2. Lisa was riding her bike home when a dog ran in front of her. She turned her bike to miss the dog, hit the curb and fell off. Sarah broke her arm.
  - Discuss these questions with your students:
    - Who caused Bart's problem? Who caused Lisa's problem?
    - Could Lisa have done anything to avoid her problem?
    - Draw Bart doing a safer activity with his bike.
    - Who here has had a problem they couldn't avoid?
    - What could Bart have done to avoid his problem?

Decision Making

Play

- ☐ **"You Be the Judge"** Have your class practice using the "**List-Compare-Choose**" steps by presenting them with hypothetical problems. **(e.g. You want more friends. You're not doing very well in school. Your friend wants you to do something wrong. Your sister picks on you. Etc.)** Divide the class in half. Have one group "List" possible solutions. Have the other group "Compare" the possible solutions by considering their consequences. Then, have the whole class "Choose" the best solution by voting.

- ☐ **"The Wisest Tribe"** Create a "problem box" for your class. Ask your students to write tough problems they are having on pieces of paper and put them in the box without signing their names. The teacher reviews the problems and selects problems to discuss.

    Then, select a small group of students each week to play the "wisest tribe." Pose a problem to the tribe that you select from the "problem box." Give them time to figure out the best solutions using the "List-Compare-Choose" steps. Have them discuss their solution with the class. Your class can make special hats or costumes to wear when playing the "tribe."

- ☐ **"Brainstorming"** Explain that "brainstorming" is when a group of people shares ideas about solving a problem or making a good decision. As a class, use the "**List-Compare-Choose**" steps to solve problems. Every student should contributes his or her ideas and opinions.
    Ask your students these questions about each step:

    1. List: What are your choices of things to do?
       Could an adult help you with this problem?
    2. Compare: What might happen after doing each of those things?
       Would any of the choices hurt you or another person?
    3. Choose: What is the best choice?
       Why is that one the best choice?

    To finish, have your students vote on the best solution and explain their decisions.
    "Brainstorm" the following situations:
    - Your friend fell off his bike and is hurt.
    - Your friend asks you to steal something.
    - You have trouble finishing your homework.
    - You heard that a good friend said you were stupid.
    - The lunch bell just rang and you left your lunch at home.
    - You're with new friends and one of them asks you to smoke a cigarette.

- ☐ **"Knowledge Quest"** Arrange for your students to join another class for this activity (or do it outdoors at recess). Divide your class into small groups. Give each group a question to ask students in the other class. **(e.g. Who has a pet? Who was born in another country? Who has a favorite book? Who has older brothers or sisters? Etc.)** Your students need to find children who fit their question and then record their names and details. Afterwards, discuss problems children had finding the right people. What they did to solve those problems? How did they divide responsibilities?

- ☐ **"Problem Solving Magician"** Write down simple problems on slips of paper and put them in a hat. Have students take turns playing the "problem solving magician" by drawing a problem out of the hat and leading the class to a good solution using the "**List-Compare-Choose**" steps. Get a cape or top hat for the "magician" to wear.

Solving Problems! As easy as 1, 2, 3

1 **LIST your choices**
What different things can you do?

Next time you have a problem, try solving it with these 3 steps!

2 **COMPARE the choices**
What would happen if you did each one?

3 **CHOOSE the best answer**
Pick the one you think is best!

PJ and the friendly stranger

PJ was on his way home from school when a man stopped his car. He asked PJ if he wanted a ride. PJ didn't know the man, but he seemed friendly. He had a pretty cool car. PJ wanted a ride but he wasn't sure what to do.

1. LIST PJ's choices (circle *all* the things PJ *could* do)
   a. PJ could accept the ride and get in the car
   b. PJ could talk to the man to see if he is nice.
   c. PJ could run away and tell an adult.

2. COMPARE the choices (*draw a line* from each choice to *what could happen*)

Accept the ride and get in.	PJ would be safe.
Talk to see if the man is nice.	The man may hurt PJ.
Run away and tell an adult.	PJ could get in trouble for talking to a stranger.

3. CHOOSE PJ's best solution (*circle* the best answer)
   a. PJ should accept the ride and get in the car.
   b. PJ should talk to the man to see if he is nice.
   c. PJ should run away and tell an adult.

Solve your own problem

Sit with a parent. Talk about how you can solve the problems below using the three steps. Ask your parents if they ever had problems like these when they were growing up.

☆ Some classmates are playing ball during recess. You want to join them. After watching for a few minutes, no one asks you to join in.

☆ You brought a picture book to school to show your friends. You put it in your desk before lunch. When you came back, it was gone.

☆ On your way to school, your stomach starts to hurt.

Name _____ Date _____

© Copyright 2008 RoboMedia, Inc. – www.LifeSkills4Kids.com

What Can I Do?

When you have a problem, there is always more than one solution.

PJ and Lolly each have a problem to solve. Different solutions are in the balloons. Help them find the best solution. Draw a string between their hands and the best solution to each problem. **Color the picture and the balloons with the best solutions.**

Write down a problem that made you make a choice: _____
_____

Two of my choices were:

1. _____
2. _____

I chose number _____ as my best solution.

Name _____ Date _____

PARENT'S INITIALS

© Copyright 2008 RoboMedia, Inc. – www.LifeSkills4Kids.com

 # Decision Making

12. I stand up for myself when people tell me to do bad things.

Lesson Notes: These activities strengthen provide assertiveness techniques that enable children to stand up for themselves when they face peer pressure to misbehave. By building <u>self-confidence</u> and <u>assertiveness</u> they prepare children to stand up for themselves. In class, teachers should emphasize role play activities to give children real practice using these techniques with their peers.

Talk

☐ Should we do everything people tell us to do? Why or why not?
☐ Why do some people copy what other person do, even if it's bad?
☐ Do you always have a choice if someone asks you to do something dangerous? Why?
☐ What is "peer pressure"?
(When someone tries to get you to do something you wouldn't ordinarily do.)
☐ How can you avoid peer pressure?
(e.g. stay away from troublemakers, always tell your parents who you play with, etc.)
☐ How can you resist peer pressure?
(e.g. change the subject, stand up for yourself, walk away, get help, etc.)
☐ Has anyone ever dared you to do something? What?
☐ When someone dares you to do something, is it usually safe or unsafe?
☐ What would you say if a stranger asked you to smoke a cigarette?
☐ What would you say if a friend asked you to smoke a cigarette?
☐ How are the two situations different?
☐ Is it harder to say "no" to a friend or a stranger? Why?
☐ Would a real friend ever want you to do something dangerous?
☐ Why might a "friend" or older person offer to give you free cigarettes, alcohol, money or toys?
☐ Who can you talk to if a friend is pressuring you to do something bad?

Make

☐ **"Protect Yourself"** Have children make posters illustrating four ways to say "No!"
(E.g. "Change the subject!", "Stand up for yourself!", "Get away!" and "Get help!" Etc.)

☐ **"Robo Poster"** Have students make posters showing a powerful robot saying "No way!" to risky situations. Include dangers and unhealthy situations unrelated to drugs.

☐ **"Good Influence - Bad Pressure"** Ask your students for examples of good and bad ways that friends might try to influence them. (e.g. **GOOD** - being a good role model, recruiting players for games, offering encouragement and compliments, rewarding good deeds, being friendly, being honest, etc. **BAD** - challenging, daring, threatening, calling them "chicken," etc.) Have each student draw a "good influence" experience and a "bad pressure" experience they had. Ask for volunteers to talk about their pictures.

☐ **"Avoiding Trouble"** Ask students for their suggestions on how to avoid harmful or illegal situations and list their suggestions on the chalkboard. Have students make posters illustrating or documenting the various tips. (e.g. don't play with children who do harmful or illegal things, suggest activities that are safe and legal, remind friends of the rules and what happens if we don't follow them, etc.)

# Decision Making

Play

- ☐ **"Resistance Role Play"** Have your students brainstorm ways to resist peer pressure and list these on the chalkboard. Use the "How to say No Way" worksheet to spark ideas. After teacher-modeling some of the refusal skills, ask for volunteers to role play the others.

- ☐ **"Puppet People"** Make puppets to portray characters from situations below. Have small groups use them to act out the scenes. This can also be done as a role play exercise.
    - The bell rings and recess is over. Your friend keeps on playing and doesn't line up. What would happen if you decided to stay and play with your friend?
    - You and your friend are in a store. Your friend steals something. What might happen to you and your friend?
    - Your friend found a gun in his father's drawer. He says he knows it's not loaded and he just wants to show it to you. What could happen if you go along with him?

    Other situations could be:
    - An older student picks on you during recess.
    - A group of friends want you to go with them into a house that is under construction.
    - A friend of yours wants you to hide stolen cigarettes at your house.
    - A classmate wants you to do a school assignment for her.
    - Your baby sitter has a friend over to your house and tells you not to tell your parents.
    - A friend's older brother offers you a drink of something you think is alcohol.
    - A stranger asks you to get in his car.

- ☐ **"Real Life Pressure Problems"** Ask your children to share some peer pressure problems they have had. **(e.g. Other children asking them to break rules, cheat, steal, smoke, lie, etc.)** Divide the class into groups to create skits about some of these situations. With younger students, assign roles and situations to them. After practicing, have the groups perform for the class. If possible, use props and costumes. After the skits, discuss what happened by asking the following questions:
    - Who has had something like this happen to them?
    - What was the problem?
    - How was the problem worked out?
    - How else could you avoid the peer pressure?
    - How else could you resist the peer pressure?
    - Is it a good idea to talk to a trusted adult when you're pressured by friends?

- ☐ **"Radio Interview"** Do video interviews with your students while pretending that they are child TV stars. Set the mood of the interview by saying that a lot of children look up to them because they're famous. Then ask them questions like these:
    - Do you think kids should try cigarettes?
    - What would you do if a friend of yours started smoking?
    - Would you feel that you had to smoke, too?
    - What could happen to you if you were with them when they smoked?
    - Could you get into trouble if they got into trouble?

Explore other peer pressure situations with different students. **(e.g. staying out late, disobeying parents, disobeying teachers, taking things that don't belong to you, hurting other people's property, etc.)** Play the interviews for the entire class and discuss the answers.

I don't always say "Yes"

As you get older, people will ask you to do all kinds of things. Some things will be good. Some things will be bad. **If anyone tells you to do something that could hurt you or someone else, it's your job to say "No way!"**

Think about the following situations.

Decide what *you* would say or do. Circle your answers.

OK!	Your Mom tells you to wash your hands	**No Way!**
OK!	A stranger asks you to get in his car	**No Way!**
OK!	Your Dad asks you to clean up your room	**No Way!**
OK!	Your teacher tells you to read a book	**No Way!**
OK!	Your older sister tells you to go to bed	**No Way!**
OK!	Your friend tells you to smoke a cigarette	**No Way!**
OK!	A group of kids dare you to steal something	**No Way!**
OK!	Your bus driver asks you to sit down	**No Way!**
OK!	Your classmate asks you for help on a lesson	**No Way!**
OK!	Your baby sitter tells you to lie to your parents	**No Way!**

What is something that you had to say "no" to lately?
_____
_____

What happened when you said "no"?
_____
_____

Tell or write a story about a time you were proud that you said "no."

Name _____ Date _____

PARENT'S INITIALS

How to say... "No way!!!"

If someone tries to get you to do something bad, there are lots of ways to protect yourself!
Read the story and put a check next to ways to say "no" that YOU have used.
Then, talk with a parent or the class about different ways to say "no."

PJ and some friends were playing kickball after school. Everyone was getting tired when Sal said, *"Hey, I have some matches. Let's start a campfire."*

Right away, PJ said, "I don't thing that's a good idea!"

His friends said, "Come on, don't be chicken. We'll just start a small campfire, OK."

What could PJ do then?

Explain to your parent or class how PJ could try each way to say "No!" in that situation.

1. **CHANGE THE SUBJECT** - PJ could:
   - ☐ Make a joke.
   - ☐ Say he wants to finish the ball game.
   - ☐ Remind his friends how much trouble they could get in.

2. **STAND UP FOR YOURSELF** - PJ could:
   - ☐ Act surprised that his friends would do something that dangerous.
   - ☐ Say, "No, I'm not going to do it. It's dumb!"

3. **GET AWAY** - If that didn't work, PJ could:
   - ☐ Make an excuse to leave like: "I'm already late for dinner. I'm outta here."
   - ☐ Just walk away from the kids who are pressuring him saying "I'll catch up with you guys later."

4. **GET HELP** - Finally, PJ could:
   - ☐ Tell an adult what happened.
   - ☐ Ask an older brother, sister or friend to help.

Check the ways to say "no" that YOU think would work best.
Tell a story about a time you stopped a bad situation by saying "No."

Name _____ Date _____

PARENT'S INITIALS

© Copyright 2008 RoboMedia, Inc. – www.LifeSkills4Kids.com

# Decision Making

13. I know who to go to when I need help.

Lesson Notes: These activities encourage children to go to trusted adults for help with certain problems. Children familiar with community helpers (Wikipedia see <u>emergency services</u>) are more likely to rely on them for help. The lesson also reviews important techniques for dealing with emergencies.

Talk

- ☐ Who are some people who help you with problems?
- ☐ When can an adult help better than one of your friends? Why?
- ☐ Why should you go to an adult for help, even if you did something wrong?
- ☐ Can you go to any adult for help? **(only a trusted adult)** Can all adults be trusted?
- ☐ When might you ask a stranger for help? **(E.g. In an emergency. In a public place or in your school where you know you are safe. When your parents, teacher or other trusted adults are nearby. When you are in a group. Etc.)**
- ☐ How can you tell if a stranger is good or bad? **(You can't be absolutely sure. That's why it's best to ask someone you know for help. If you must ask a stranger, then be careful.)**
- ☐ Which strangers are probably OK?
  (e.g. community workers, police, firefighters, delivery people; people wearing a uniform or identification badge; clean and professional looking; etc.)
- ☐ Which strangers should you stay away from?
  (e.g. anyone who asks you to go with them alone; who invites you to an unfamiliar place like their car, woods, building, alley, etc.; asks you to let them in your home when your parents aren't there; offers you candy, toys, food, or money for no reason; looks dirty or acts strange; etc.)
- ☐ If you meet a suspicious stranger, what should you do? **(Run away and tell a trusted adult.)**
- ☐ What is an "emergency"? **(a sudden, unexpected event requiring immediate action)**
- ☐ Why would you get help in an emergency?

Make

- ☐ **"My Adult Friend"** Draw a picture of a trusted adult with this title. Talk about how trusted adults and family members are considered "friends", too. Be sure to show them your picture.
- ☐ **"MDM Team"** Have your students make buttons, ribbons, armbands or t-shirts saying "I'm part of the *Million Dollar Machine Team!*" Each student makes 2; one for him or her self and one to give to a trusted adult. Have students wear the items on a special day.
- ☐ **"Support Your Local Police"** Have your students send pictures and letters to local law enforcement groups. The messages can be "We know we can count on you!"; "Thanks for making our neighborhood safe!"; "The kids at _____ E.S. love you!"; etc. The class could also work together on one large card or poster.
- ☐ **"Harmonious Helpers"** Have children draw different community helpers we all share. Write a simple description of each helper on the back. Use the same rhythm to aid memorization. **(e.g. policeman - "keeps my neighborhood safe"; doctor - "cures me when I'm sick"; mother - "loves me all the time"; bus driver - "gets me to school on time"; teacher - "helps me learn and grow"; etc.)** Hold up pictures of the helpers and quiz students on their duties.
- ☐ **"Helpers Together"** Have your students name types of people who are part of their personal help network. **(e.g. Mom, Dad, brother, sister, teacher, religious leader, relatives, teacher, nurse, doctor, police person, etc.)** Then, have them draw 5 important helpers together in one imaginary scene. **(e.g. as members in a band, eating dinner together, riding in a convertible, etc.)**

Decision Making

- ☐ **"Local Heroes"** Using newspaper and magazine pictures or drawings, make a class collage of different community professionals who are there to help us. **(e.g. police officers, fire fighters, nurses, doctors, paramedics, utility workers, counselors, etc.)** Discuss ways that each professional can help us.

- ☐ **"Emergency Training"** Invite the school nurse to talk to your class about what to do when confronted by different medical emergencies.

- ☐ **"Home Safety"** Have students name some emergencies that can occur at home. **(e.g. small child swallows a poison, father cuts hand working in garage, fire starts on stove, friend falls down steps and hits head, etc.)** List these on the board. Have students make up safety posters with tips on what to do if the emergency occurs.

- ☐ **"How I Helped"** Have students draw an emergency they saw. Ask for volunteers to talk about what they did to help. Ask them if they would do anything different next time. Students who can't think of an emergency can draw one they saw on TV and describe how people reacted.

Play

- ☐ **"Telephone Expert"** Train children to use the **911 emergency phone number** with the "In Case of Emergency" worksheet. If possible, bring a touch-tone phone, rotary phone and different cell phones to class to have children practice dialing emergency numbers. Then have them role play how to report various emergency situations. See the Wikipedia article on 911.

- ☐ **"Big Help"** Have students assemble a collection of pictures showing people helping each other and pictures of people <u>not</u> helping each other. Have children sort the pictures of people helping from the pictures of people not helping as they explain the differences.

- ☐ **"Singing Helper-Gram"** Walk your class through the school to meet the nurse, principal, secretary, counselor, etc. Have students sing the song below to the tune of "Farmer in the Dell." Repeat the song substituting the names of other helpers.

  > "The nurse is my friend, the nurse is my friend!
  > "She's always there to help me out, the nurse is my friend!"

- ☐ **"Helper Dress-Up"** Assemble a collection of props and costumes representing various community helpers. **(e.g. teachers, school counselor, school nurse, family members, police officers, doctors, adult friends, etc.)** Then, have children role play the situations below. One possible helper is suggested for each situation.
    - You have a bad cold. **(nurse)**
    - You don't understand a math problem. **(teacher)**
    - You get lost in a big store. **(sales clerk)**
    - A classmate brings a knife to school. **(teacher)**
    - You don't want to walk across the street alone. **(crossing guard)**
    - A friend wants you to smoke a cigarette. **(parent)**
    - A stranger asks you to get in their car. **(police)**
    - Your mom faints. **(neighbor)**
    - A bad dog chases you on the way home from school. **(parent)**
    - You step on a nail. **(doctor)**

- ☐ **"Field Trip"** Organize a class field trip to a hospital, police station or firehouse. Prepare a list of questions to ask before you go. **(e.g. How do they handle different emergencies? What special training do they have? How do we contact them for help? Etc.)**

Name _____
Date _____

PARENT'S INITIALS

Who can help?

You solve lots of your own problems, but *sometimes* you need help. Who do you go to when you have a tough problem? People on your team will help! Read the problems below. <u>Draw lines</u> from each problem to people who can help you solve it. Some problems have more than one person who can help.

 Parent

 Policeman

 Teacher

You move to a new town and you feel lonely.

You can't close the zipper on your jacket.

A classmate is telling lies about you.

You need help fixing your bike.

You don't feel well in school.

You see people breaking into a car.

You see smoke coming out of a house.

You're having trouble with your work in school.

Two older kids take your lunchbox away from you.

You see some kids breaking windows at your school.

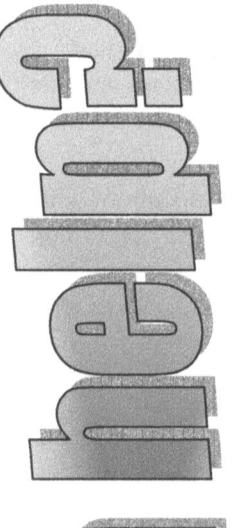 School Nurse

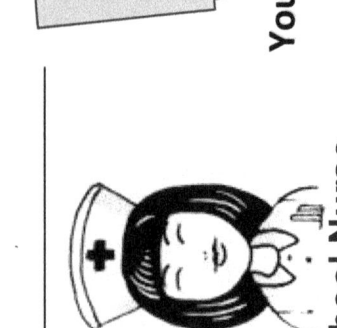 Older Brother or Sister

 Fireman

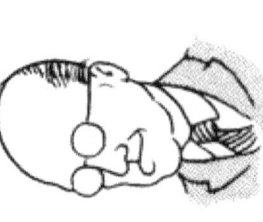 Principal

© Copyright 2008 RoboMedia, Inc. – www.LifeSkills4Kids.com

In Case of Emergency

Emergencies don't happen often. But if an emergency does happen, knowing what to do and how to get help can save lives. The most important tool in an emergency is a **telephone**. Show your parent that you know how to dial emergency numbers on each of the phones on the left and that you know what to say.

FILL THIS IN WITH YOUR PARENTS AND TAPE IT BY THE PHONE

WHO TO CALL FOR HELP!!!

	NUMBER
Police	___ - ___ - _____
Neighbor	___ - ___ - _____
Operator	___ - ___ - _____
Parent at work	___ - ___ - _____
Parent cell phone	___ - ___ - _____
Fire Department	___ - ___ - _____
Poison Control Center	___ - ___ - _____
Ambulance	___ - ___ - _____

HOW TO CALL FOR HELP!

1. STAY CALM
2. Wait for the dial tone, then Dial "911" or the correct number above.
3. Tell the emergency person <u>what is wrong.</u>
4. Then Say,
   "My name is _____"
   "My address is _____"
   "My telephone number is _____"

Don't hang up until the emergency person hangs up.

Standard Telephone Dial 1920s - 1980s

© 2008 RoboMedia, Inc. – www.LifeSkills4Kids.com

Name _____ Date _____

PARENT'S INITIALS

Decision Making

14. I must protect my body from dangerous things.

Lesson Notes: These activities focus on poisons and dangerous situations your children may encounter. If your school has a home safety curriculum, these activities will reinforce and expand its concepts. Scientific evaluations show measurable improvement in these safety skills among children using the Million Dollar Machine Program. This lesson is a good introduction to Lesson 18, which covers the dangers of tobacco, alcohol and other drugs exclusively. For more resources visit the Home Safety Council website at MySafeHome.org.

Talk

- What are some things you have to protect your *Million Dollar Machine* from? **(e.g. drugs, poison, strangers, cars, bicycle accidents, guns, electricity, fire, etc.)**
- Who are some of the people who help you protect your Million *Dollar Machine*? **(e.g. parents, teacher, police, President of the U.S., school bus driver, etc.)**
- How do your parents help you protect your *Million Dollar Machine*?
- Are your parents always with you?
- Who protects your *Million Dollar Machine* when your parents aren't around? **(the child)**
- Why is it always your job to protect your *Million Dollar Machine*?
- What does toxic mean? What is a poison? See the Wikipedia article on poison.
- Can something safe become a poison if used improperly?
- How could eating too much of your favorite food be bad?
- How can you tell the difference between things that are good for you and things that are not?
- If you can't tell the difference, who can you ask for help?

Make

- **"Safety Tips"** Have students suggest safety tips for the home. Use the "Safety Detective" worksheet to spark ideas. Have students make posters illustrating specific tips.

- **"Things to Watch Out For!"** Have your students make a bulletin board with pictures of dangerous and toxic substances. Have them illustrate the risks posed by each substance. **(e.g. cleaning fluid - burns eyes; gasoline - starts fires; eating paste – sick stomach, etc.)**

- **"Adult Use Only"** Explain that some household items are safe for adults to use but aren't safe for children. **(e.g. knives, lawn mower, power tools, bleach, gasoline, cleanser, medicine, etc.)** Ask students to draw or find pictures of some of these unsafe things.

- **"My Safe House"** Have children create a large bulletin board drawing of a house, showing different rooms. Divide your class into groups and assign a different room to each. Have the groups show hazardous items, like those below, with ideas on how to store and use them safely. See "Safety Detective" worksheet and MySafeHome.org for ideas.
    - **Bathroom** - nail polish and remover, hair spray, cleaning products, lotion, razors, medicines, slippery surfaces, electrical appliances
    - **Kitchen** - oven cleaner, dishwashing detergent, cleaning products, matches, garbage disposal, knives, range/oven, electrical appliances
    - **Garage** - gasoline, insecticides, paints, tools, car, electrical box
    - **Utility room** - detergent, bleach, cleaning supplies, iron

Decision Making

- ☐ **"Stay Away from Mr. Yuk"** Introduce the "Mr. Yuk" symbol to your students. Explain that containers with this symbol have dangerous things inside. Emphasize that children should never eat or drink anything from a "Mr. Yuk" container. Give them circle patterns to trace on green construction paper. Have them cut out the circles and draw "Mr. Yuk" faces with a black marker. Have students take the faces home and, with their parents' help, tape them on unsafe substances. See the Wikipedia article on Mr. Yuk and links to the Mr. Yuk homepage.
- ☐ **"Safe Choice"** Have children draw pictures of healthy products **(e.g. milk, produce, cereal, etc.)** and products that could poison them **(e.g. tobacco, drain cleaner, bug spray, etc.).** Put "Mr. Yuk" symbols on the appropriate products.

Play

- ☐ **"Locked Up Tight"** Have students cut pictures from magazines of over-the-counter medicines, household chemicals and cleaners. Make a "medicine cabinet" and a "locked pantry" out of two large boxes. Have students place pictures in the appropriate boxes.
- ☐ **"Safety Inspector"** Have children name dangerous situations they might find at home and how to correct the situations. **(e.g. discover door to pantry open - lock door so younger sister can't get in; discover spilled gasoline in garage - get parent; discover bug spray in medicine cabinet - give spray to adult to put in proper place; discover young child playing with electrical outlet - supervise child or get an adult, etc.)** In groups, have them role play the part of "Safety Inspector" discovering one of the situations and handling it properly. For younger children, you may want to assign situations. Students can wear a badge or hat during the role play.
- ☐ **"Safety is in the Bag"** Assemble a collection of pictures of safe and unsafe things (or actual empty containers **that have been cleaned well**). Put them in a large, opaque bag. Place two boxes -- one labeled with a happy face and the other with a "Mr. Yuk" face at the front of the class. Have each child take one object or picture out of the bag and place it in the proper box while explaining his or her decision.
- ☐ **"Pill Problem"** Get a pair of student volunteers. Have one role play a young child playing with a bottle of pills. Have the other role play an older child who discovers the situation and explains the danger to the younger child. Have the rest of the class observe the interaction and comment on what went on. Substitute new situations for subsequent pairs of students. **(e.g. razor, electrical outlet, matches, pack of cigarettes, lighter, loose pills that look like candy, etc.)**
- ☐ **"Visitor"** Invite a firefighter or rescue worker to talk to your class about home safety. Have students come up with questions beforehand to get the conversation started.

Safety Detective

Dear Parent,

This week, we're studying household safety. Many accidents that happen at home can be prevented. Please go through this safety checklist with your child and talk about ways you keep your home safe.

Does our home have these important safety features?

- ❑ Our stairs are well lit and have handrails.
- ❑ Our rugs are fastened down so we don't trip.
- ❑ We have smoke detectors with fresh batteries.
- ❑ Children's bedroom windows are labeled for firefighters.

Are we careful with electricity?

- ❑ We don't use electricity near water.
- ❑ We don't overload electric receptacles.
- ❑ There are no frayed wires on our appliances.
- ❑ We have safety caps on electrical outlets where small children play.

Are dangerous things stored properly?

- ❑ We don't store poisonous substances near food.
- ❑ We keep our cleaning supplies out of reach of small children and pets.
- ❑ We store dangerous substances, like paint and gasoline, properly.
- ❑ We keep knives, razors and power tools out of reach of small children.

Is our bathroom safe?

- ❑ We keep all medicines in their original, labeled containers.
- ❑ We flush outdated medicines down the toilet.
- ❑ We keep our hot water heater set at 120 degrees to avoid burns.
- ❑ We have a non-slip surface in the bathtub.

Does everyone know what to do in an emergency?

- ❑ We have a list of emergency numbers near our phone.
- ❑ Every member of our family knows what to do in an emergency.

Name _____ Date _____

PARENT'S INITIALS

© Copyright 2008 RoboMedia, Inc. – www.LifeSkills4Kids.com

Safe or Not Safe?

One day after school, you were visiting a friend. Your friend's Dad just came home from the store with some packages. He was putting things away when he got a phone call. He went to another room and left you, your friend, and your friend's baby sister in the kitchen. Decide which things you think are unsafe in the kitchen and which are safe.

Circle safe items

Put an "X" over unsafe items

Talk about these questions with your parents:

Why isn't it safe to leave prescription pills out in the open?
Where is the safest place to store medicine?
Where should knives be stored?

Why is it unsafe for the insect spray to be left out?
Where should it be kept?
What could happen if the stove is left on?

You can make the rooms in your house safer. Check your house with your parents. Fix any unsafe situations you find.

PARENT'S INITIALS

Name _____ Date _____

© 2008 RoboMedia, Inc. – www.LifeSkills4Kids.com

Drug Awareness

15. Cigarettes, alcohol and other drugs hurt the body.

Lesson Notes: The MDM lessons teach that tobacco, alcohol and other drugs are always harmful to children. This lesson teaches children that the best way to avoid drug problems is to never try drugs.

The activities put special emphasis on the proven harmful effects of tobacco and alcohol. MDM's authors and educational consultants view tobacco and alcohol as the most common gateway drugs to a drug using lifestyle. Tobacco and alcohol use initiates children into many negative activities, preparing them for continued and diversified drug use. These include: lying to parents; concealing contraband; concealing the activity; covering up symptoms such as dizziness and breath, hand or clothing odor; stealing; disregarding authority and rules; and intentionally damaging the body.

Talk

- ☐ What are drugs? (In this curriculum, "drug" means tobacco, alcohol, all illegal substances and any medicine that is abused.)
- ☐ What is the difference between drugs and medicines?
- ☐ Can a safe medicine ever become a harmful drug?
  (e.g. if too much is used, taken at wrong time, taken without doctor or parent's permission, etc.)
- ☐ What are some drugs that hurt the *Million Dollar Machine*?
- ☐ How do each of these drugs hurt the *Million Dollar Machine*?
- ☐ What does "illegal" mean? Why are all drugs illegal for children?
- ☐ Are drugs bad for adults, too?
- ☐ Why might an adult use a drug they know is bad for them?
- ☐ Why are drugs even more dangerous for children than adults?
- ☐ What is the difference between snuff, cigarettes and chewing tobacco?
- ☐ Are they all harmful?
- ☐ Were cigarettes and alcohol ever advertised on TV? Are they now? Why or why not? (Wikipedia see alcohol advertising)
- ☐ Why are harmful drugs like tobacco and alcohol still advertised in some places?
- ☐ If a person dies using any type of drug, who is to blame?

Make

- ☐ **"Drugs are Dangerous!"** Have your students make posters warning people about the dangers of using alcohol, tobacco and other drugs. Include caffeine as a drug children shouldn't expose themselves to.

- ☐ **"Choosing Sides"** Pair your students. Have each pair trace a body outline on butcher paper and draw a line down the middle. On one side, have them draw healthy organs (**brain, heart, lungs, stomach, kidneys and liver**). On the other side, have them draw what they think organs that have been damaged by tobacco, alcohol or other drugs might look like.

- ☐ **"These help me grow! These make me slow!"** Make a bulletin board with this theme. Have your students find magazine ads showing healthy and unhealthy products and activities. Attach the pictures to the appropriate side of the board.

- ☐ **"Warning! Don't Smoke or Drink!"** Have students find the different warnings that appear on cigarettes, alcoholic beverages and their ads. Have your school nurse or drug education coordinator visit your class to discuss each warning. Establish that cigarettes and alcohol are never legal for children to use. Ask them if they think this is a good idea and why.

Drug Awareness

- ☐ **"Truth in Advertising"** Find magazine ads for alcohol and tobacco products. Discuss how the ads try to make smoking and drinking look like a good thing. **(e.g. shows healthy people, makes it look fun or exciting, etc.)** What effects do smoking and drinking really have on our health? Discuss why the ads don't show these bad things?

- ☐ **"The Real Message"** Have students cut out magazine ads for cigarettes and alcohol. Paste the ads onto poster boards and then draw or print harmful effects of the drugs around the ads. **(e.g. people reacting to the smoke, the smoker going to the doctor, smelly breath, starting a fire, brown teeth, out of breath, bad gums, etc.)** Create a true headline for each poster. (e.g. "Cigarettes make lungs black!", "Alcohol stops children from growing up healthy!", etc.)

- ☐ Teacher Web Resources: Visit the American Lung Association at www.LungUSA.org for the "Smoking 101 Fact Sheet" and more; the Partnership for a Drug Free America is a terrific resource at www.DrugFree.org; and the Indiana Prevention Resource Center at www.drugs.indiana.edu has facts about all types of drugs, PDF downloads, PowerPoint presentations, articles and much more.

Play

- ☐ **"Circle of Knowledge"** Seat students in a circle. Play recorded music as they pass a ball around the circle. When the music stops, the child with the ball tells something that he or she knows about alcohol, tobacco or other drugs. Other students can add facts by raising their hands. The student with the ball selects one of them to speak and then passes the ball. If no one has anything to add, resume the music.

- ☐ **"The Best Defense"** Ask pairs of students to volunteer for this role play. One student pretends to be a harmful substance **(e.g. beer, pill, cigarette, etc.)** coaxing the second student into allowing the substance to enter his or her body. The second student defends his or her body from the drug by resisting verbally. **(e.g. No way!, you can hurt my lungs, you can make me sick, I'd rather read, leave me alone, I'm telling my Mom, etc.)**

- ☐ **"Better Idea"** Divide your class into two teams. Alternate sides and ask students to come up with positive alternatives to using drugs. Keep going until students run out of ideas and declare it a tie. You may wish to have students draw some of the positive alternatives to drugs.

- ☐ **"Ad Actor"** Set up role plays where children act like characters in magazine ads for cigarettes or alcohol. Have them act out what the person in the ad might *really* be saying or thinking. **(e.g. These cigarettes smell; I only smoke in these ads because they pay me a lot of money; I feel sick; I feel guilty telling people to drink; I wonder if this is hurting my body?; etc.)**

- ☐ **"Health Visitor"** Invite a health professional to talk to your class about how drugs affect the body's normal functions. Ensure that the visitor's message will be compatible with the zero-use message of this curriculum. Brief the guest in advance about the concept that the *"Million Dollar Machine"* is what your children call the human body. If possible, share this lesson plan with the speaker before their visit.

- ☐ **"Student Visitor"** Invite an older student from your school **(2 to 3 grades ahead of your class is best)** to talk to your students about resisting drug problems. **(e.g. coping with peer pressure, avoiding people who smoke, turning down drugs, etc.)** In advance, review topics with the student and how they relate to your lesson. Encourage the student to present real life stories about facing and successfully avoiding or resisting drug use situations.

There's more than one path through life. You can take the road of good food, exercise and rest so your body grows up healthy. Some people take other roads that lead to dead ends. **Help PJ find his way to HEALTH.**
Watch out for dead ends!

Name_____ Date _____

PARENT'S INITIALS

Facts about Alcohol and Tobacco

Help Lolly and PJ understand how alcohol and tobacco hurt the body

Complete these sentences about alcohol.

Word Bank:	healthy	alcohol	drug	illegal

- Beer, wine, and liquor all contain _____.
- Alcohol is a _____.
- Alcohol is not _____ for anyone.
- Alcohol is _____ for children.

Complete these sentences about tobacco:

Word Bank:	illegal	healthy	harmful	nicotine

- The tobacco plant contains a drug called _____.
- Cigarettes, snuff, and chewing tobacco are all _____.
- Tobacco products are not _____ for anyone.
- Tobacco products are _____ for children.

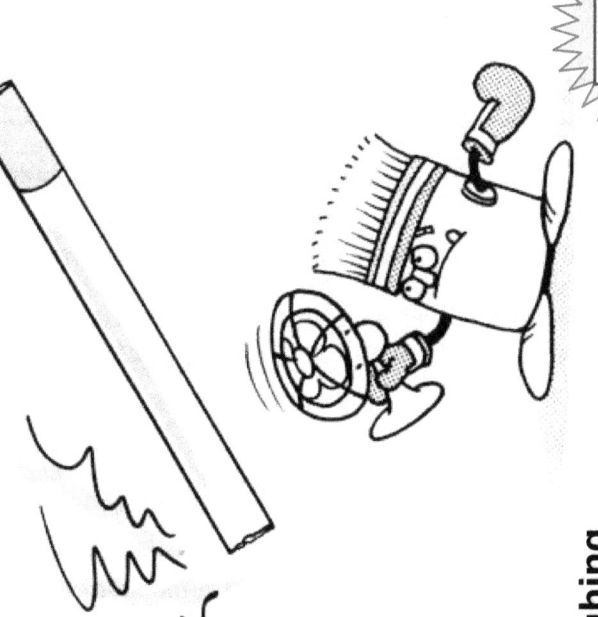

Alcohol and tobacco cause many problems. Draw an arrow from the problem to the drug that causes it. Some of the problems are caused by alcohol <u>and</u> tobacco.

- Burns you
- Is addictive
- Is expensive
- Makes you dizzy
- Hurts your heart
- Makes you sleepy
- Upsets your stomach
- Makes you gain weight
- Makes your breath smell
- Hurts your teeth and gums
- Hurts your lungs and causes coughing

PARENT'S INITIALS

Name _____ Date _____

© Copyright 2008 RoboMedia, Inc. — www.LifeSkills4Kids.com

Drug Awareness

16. Only a doctor, nurse or my parents can give me medicine.

Lesson Notes: These exercises examine the differences between "drugs*" and medicine. They establish that doctors are highly trained professionals who use medicine only under special circumstances. Learning to distinguish between appropriate and inappropriate use of medicine strengthens children's ability to identify and resist harmful drug use.
* **In this curriculum the term "drug" means any substances that are illegal and harmful for children, including alcohol and tobacco which are legal for adults.**

Talk
- ☐ What is "medicine"? What does medicine look like? Name some medicines.
- ☐ Why do doctors sometimes give us medicine? **(see "Healing Tools" activity below)**
- ☐ Why is it safe for a doctor or your parents to give us medicine?
- ☐ Who else could help you take your medicine? Who are people who can NOT give us medicine?
- ☐ What are some differences <u>prescription medicine</u> and <u>over-the-counter</u> medicines?
- ☐ What is an "<u>over-the-counter</u>" medicine? **(Medicines like cough syrup, aspirin, vitamins, antiseptic, sinus spray, etc. which don't require a doctor's prescription to buy.)**
- ☐ Do over-the-counter medicines come from a safe place? Why?
- ☐ What are some differences between "medicine" and "drugs"?
- ☐ Can a healing medicine become a harmful drug?
- ☐ What could make a helpful medicine harmful?
  (e.g. using too much, taking at the wrong time, mixing with other medicines, taking someone else's medicine, not having adult supervision, medicine too old, not following directions, etc.)
- ☐ Would you share your medicine with a friend? Why not?
- ☐ What are some things other than medicine that can make a person feel better?
  (e.g. rest, fresh air, exercise, playing a game, spending time with a friend, eating a good meal, etc.)

Make
- ☐ **"Many Medicines"** Have your school nurse or drug abuse coordinator talk to your class about different forms that medicine comes in. **(e.g. capsules, liquids, tablets, inhalants, injections, ointments, patches, etc.)** If possible, show an example of each form of medicine. Discuss how some medicines look like candy. Relate this to the danger of accepting candy from a stranger. After the discussion, have students draw different forms of medicine.
- ☐ **"Medicine Safety Looks Like This"** Have children draw pictures of people using medicine safely. **(e.g. measuring dosage, looking at clock, reading labels, adult giving to child, keeping in medicine cabinet, etc.)** Visit <u>FDA.gov</u> and search "Use Medicine Safely" for a helpful article and PDF.
- ☐ **"Healing Tools"** Explain that doctors use medicine to help people in only the 4 situations listed below. Have your students talk about a time their doctor gave them medicine. Relate their experiences to the 4 situations.
  Then, divide a bulletin board into 4 sections and have students put pictures or drawings of appropriate medicines in each area.
  - o To prevent disease (e.g. vaccine, vitamin)
  - o To stop pain or discomfort (e.g. aspirin, Novocain)
  - o To cure disease (e.g. antibiotic)
  - o To correct chemical imbalances (e.g. insulin)

Drug Awareness

- **"School Medicine Safety Rules"** Have the school nurse visit to explain the school rules for taking medicine. Ask students why they think each rule has been included. Have students make a poster of the rules for classroom display. Modify these rules to match your school:
    - You always need a note from your parents.
    - The medicine bottle must be labeled with your name.
    - The bottle must tell when and how to take the medicine, and how much to take.
    - The adult in charge of the medicine is the only one who gives it.

- **"Home Medicine Safety Rules"** Have students name medicine safety rules like those below and then make a poster with this theme for classroom display:
    - Always follow your doctor's directions for taking the medicine.
    - Always read the medicine's directions carefully and follow them.
    - Never take medicine without an adult's supervision.
    - Never take someone else's medicine.
    - Keep all medicines in a safe place.
    - Flush outdated medicines down the toilet.

Play

- **"Medical Team"** Have 4 students dress like doctors and set up an "office" in front of the class. Ask volunteers to think of times they had to take medicine and to visit the "doctors" to be interviewed. Each "doctor" asks a specific question about the sick student's experience. (e.g. Who told you to take the medicine? What did the medicine look or taste like? Why did you need the medicine? What happened when you took the medicine? Etc.)

- **"I Know What's Not For Me"** Have students bring in food containers from home. The teacher or nurse provides cleaned containers of prescription and non-prescription medicines, household cleaners, cigarettes, vitamins, etc. Set all these items on a table with the food containers. Quiz children about which items could hurt them. Have them place these items in a box or garbage can labeled "Not For Me."

- **"Musical Questions"** Set up a row of chairs at the front of the room. Label the back of each chair with the name of a food, drug, medicine or harmful substance. Have small groups of children come to the front of the room. Play music as they walk around the chairs. When you stop the music, the children sit down. Select students to answer these questions about the item on the back of their chair:
    - Is this item ever safe to use?
    - Who could tell you to use this item?
    - How could this item hurt you if it was used improperly?

- **"My Visit to the Doctor"** Ask students to role play visits to the doctor, school nurse and dentist. Have the student playing the health professional dispense a medicine during some of the visits. Have the students demonstrate the proper use of the medicine and explain why the professional prescribed the medicine in each case.

- **"Good For You May Be Bad For Me"** Have children role play situations where one sick child offers his or her medicine to another child with similar symptoms. Have the second child refuse the medicine and explain why it wouldn't be a healthy thing to do.

- **"Pharmacy Field Trip"** Arrange a field trip to a local pharmacy when the pharmacist has time to talk to your class about his or her job.

"I know about medicine"

You know that only a doctor, nurse or your parents can give you medicine.

Sit with your parents and talk about each of the following situations. Tell your parents what you think is the right thing to do in each case.

- When Keisha's dad has an upset stomach, he eats little pink mints. Keisha's dad gave them to her once when she had an upset stomach. They tasted really good.
- Should Keisha eat more mints?

- Sue had a cold with a bad cough. Her doctor gave her cherry syrup that made the cough go away.
- Two weeks later, her brother got the cold, probably from her. Sue offered her brother the syrup to help his cough. Should he take it?

- Sally's mom gives her a vitamin every day. She says it helps Sally to grow and be strong.
- Sally thinks that she would grow faster if she took more vitamins. Should she?

- When Alan has a headache, his mom gives him an aspirin.
- Today he has a headache, but his mom is busy working outside. Should he get his own aspirin?

- Bill's Cub Scout pack was going camping. Bill has been sick for days. His mom said he couldn't go unless he was better.
- The day of the trip, Bill took twice as much of his medicine so that he would feel better. Did Bill do the right thing?

PARENT'S INITIALS

Name _____ Date _____

© 2008 RoboMedia, Inc. – www.LifeSkills4Kids.com

Health Helpers

Read the list below. **Circle the people who are allowed to give you each item.** You can circle 1, 2 or 3 people. Cross out people who shouldn't give that item to you.

In the first example, you wouldn't take aspirin from your friend but it is OK from either a doctor or your parent. Do the rest on your own. **Talk to a parent about your choices.**

	Your Doctor	Your parent	Your friend
Aspirin	⭕	⭕	❌
Cough syrup			
Pills			
Glass of water			
Cigarette			
Band-Aid			
Needle			

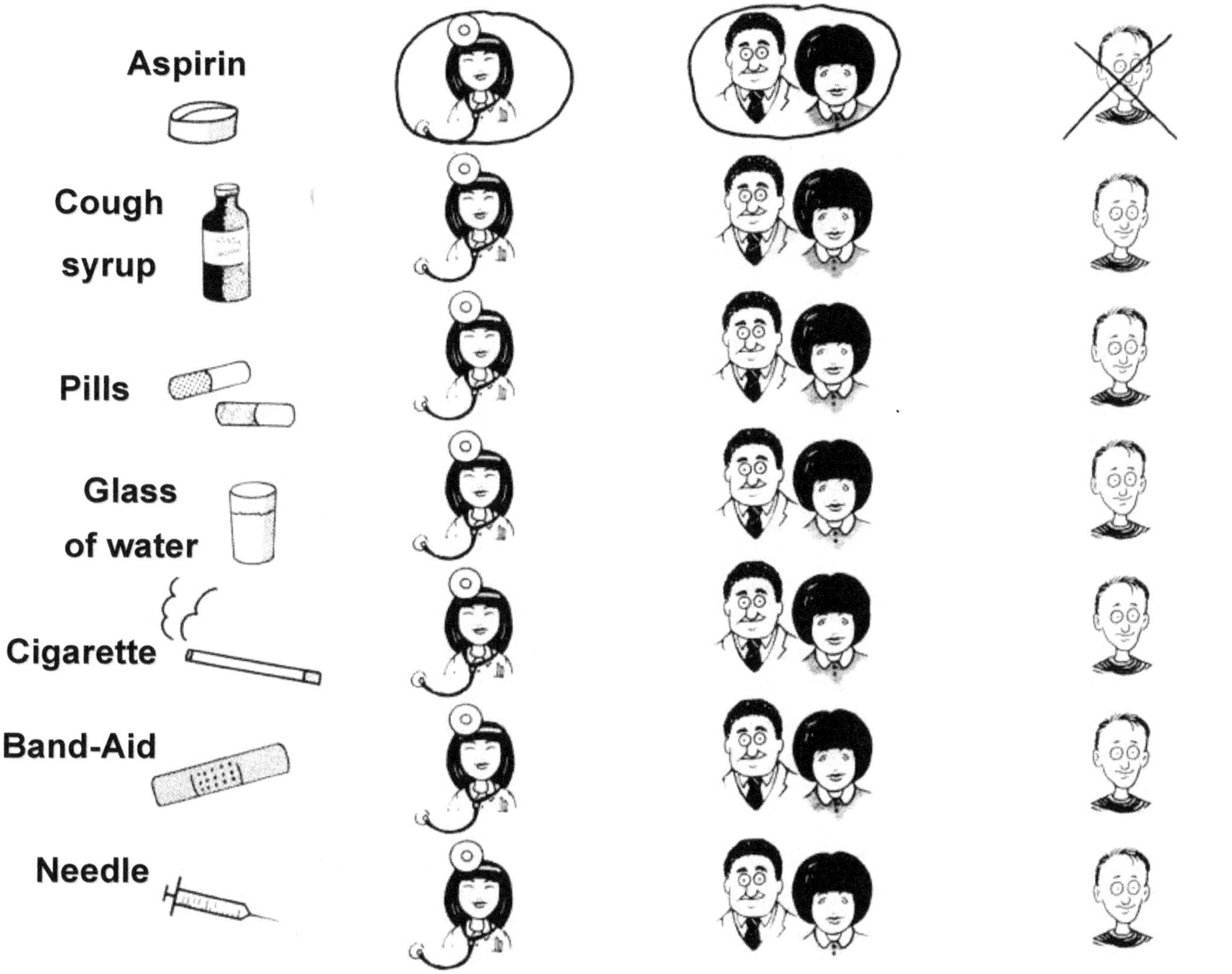

Discuss these questions with a parent:

1. Why did you circle the people you did?
2. Why did you cross out the people you did?
3. Why can a doctor give you things that your parents can not give you?

Name_____ Date_____

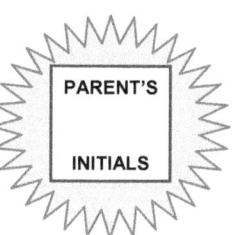

PARENT'S INITIALS

© 2008 RoboMedia, Inc. – www.LifeSkills4Kids.com

Drug Awareness

17. It's not my fault someone I love uses tobacco, alcohol or drugs.

Lesson Notes: Be sensitive to the fact that many children have family members who use tobacco, alcohol or other drugs. This lesson helps children realize that a parent or relative's drug problem is never their fault. To create a healing environment, it is important not to place blame on the drug user. Do not give students the message that people who use drugs are bad. Help students distinguish between the behavior (**drug use in this case**) and the person who is engaging in the behavior. Rather than condemn a person with <u>drug addiction</u>, children must learn to help them.

Talk

- ☐ Why is it normal to feel bad if someone you love uses drugs?
- ☐ Why isn't it your fault if someone you love uses drugs?
  (e.g. they started before you were born, their decision, you didn't tell them to use the drug, etc.)
- ☐ Why might an adult use tobacco, alcohol or other drugs?
  (e.g. copied friends, started when young, didn't realize harm to body, addicted, etc.)
- ☐ When someone uses a drug for a long time, can they stop easily?
- ☐ Why is it hard to stop using these drugs?
- ☐ What can happen when a person tries to stop using drugs?
  (e.g. person may feel sick, tired, angry, sad, nervous, tense, etc.)
- ☐ What kinds of problems can happen in a family with a drug user?
  (e.g. bad communication; no family activities; physical violence; lack of money, cleanliness, good meals, supervision; bad people coming to house, etc.)
- ☐ If someone in your family has a drug problem, which family members can help fix it? **(everyone)**
- ☐ What can family members do to help a member with a drug problem?
  (e.g. get help, love them, be gentle, don't yell at them, encourage them to stop, etc.)
- ☐ Do we ever need help from outside our family to solve problems?
  (e.g. whenever we need a specialist like a doctor, auto mechanic, electrician, etc.)
- ☐ Who can you talk to if someone in your family has a drug problem?
  (e.g. parent, relative, teacher, school nurse, religious leader, etc.)
- ☐ Who are some "specialists" who help solve drug problems? **(e.g. family counselor, drug "hotline," drug treatment center workers, social workers, etc.)**

Make

- ☐ **"Household Helper"** Have children draw themselves helping adult family members with household chores. Discuss many other ways that children can help adults.
- ☐ **"My Family Friend"** Have your students draw themselves getting help from someone outside their home. **(e.g. grandparent, teacher, clergy, relative, etc.)**
  "Healing Helpers" Have your students draw places and people who could help solve a drug use problem. **(e.g. hospital and doctor, church and pastor, office and nurse or counselor, school and teacher, home and relative, etc.)**

Drug Awareness

- ☐ **"I Care About You"** Have your students make "caring cards" for all the adult members of their families. Suggest message like "I care about you," "If you ever have a problem, I hope I can help you," "I'm proud that you are my parent." Etc.

- ☐ **"Drug Solutions"** Have your students suggest ways to help a family member with a drug problem. Discuss ways that students can get help for themselves and members of their families. **(e.g. school counselor, religious leader, school nurse, drug education or treatment organization, parents, older brother or sister, etc.)** Make a class poster showing the different adults who could help in this situation.

- ☐ Teacher resource: Use Google.com to search Getting help for drug addiction. Excellent resources include DrugFree.org, HelpGuide.org and About.com.

Play

- ☐ **"Doing My Part"** Demonstrate the importance of family team work.
    - ○ **With a blanket** - Have a group of students hold a blanket by the edges to form a flat surface. Assign a different family role to each group member. Put a ball on the blanket. Tell students to move the ball to different locations without letting it fall off. During the action of moving the ball, tell some students to let go of the blanket while others keep trying to accomplish the task.
    - ○ **With yarn** - Have a group of children hold a long piece of yarn that has been tied into a loop. Have children pull the yarn to form specific geometric shapes. **(e.g. circle, square, rectangle, triangle, etc.)** Then, instruct some children to keep holding the yarn but not to cooperate with their teammates.

    After these activities, discuss what happened when team members didn't cooperate with each other. Discuss problems caused by a student stopping unexpectedly. Explain that families need teamwork, too. When one member of a family doesn't help, certain things don't get done. Relate this to a family with one member who has a problem with alcohol or other drugs. Talk about how the whole family is affected.

- ☐ **"Everybody's Problem"** Have children create role play skits showing problems caused by a drug using family member. **(e.g. drinking too much on vacation family member becomes sick; smoker bothers family at restaurant; drinking too much at night family member can't drive child to school function, etc.)**

    After each problem is presented, have the rest of the class use the **3 Steps to Solving Problems (see Lesson 11)** to arrive at the best solution. Then, have the players finish the skit based on the class choice.

- ☐ **"Family Specialist"** Invite a family counselor to talk to your class about how they help families. Make sure to discuss problems and solutions related to drug use and that the visitor's message is be compatible with the "zero-drug-use for children" message of this curriculum. Brief the guest in advance about the concept that the *"Million Dollar Machine"* is what your children call the human body. If possible, share this lesson plan with the speaker before their visit.

It's not your fault!

Dear Parent: Please read this story to your child and discuss the questions at the bottom. The story helps your child understand that it's not their fault when an adult uses a drug. It also explains how difficult it is for a person to stop using a drug.

This story is about Butch and his Mom. Butch's Mom used to smoke cigarettes even though she knew smoking was bad for her health. One morning, Butch's Mom decided to quit. After a few hours, she really wanted a cigarette but she didn't let herself have one. Later that day, she began to feel sick and tense.

Butch came home from school. He tried to tell his Mom about a special visitor that they had that day. His Mom felt so sick that she was mean to Butch. She said she didn't want to hear about it. She sent Butch outside to play. Butch was hurt. He thought he had done something wrong. He thought it was his fault that his Mom was angry.

The next day Butch talked to his teacher. His teacher explained that Butch's Mom wasn't mad at Butch. She told him that his Mom was addicted to cigarettes. When you try to stop smoking cigarettes you feel sick for awhile. This can make you say things you don't really mean.

That day Butch went home and talked to his Mom. He told her what his teacher said. Butch's Mom agreed. She hugged Butch and said she was sorry she yelled at him. She said she wasn't mad at him.

After a few more days, Butch's Mom felt better. She was happy she had stopped smoking cigarettes. Butch knew that she made a healthy decision. That made Butch feel better, too.

Discussion Questions:

1. Why did Butch's Mom feel sick?
2. Why was Butch unhappy?
3. Did Butch do anything wrong?
4. Why was it hard for Butch's Mom to stop smoking cigarettes?
5. If a parent smokes cigarettes, is it their child's fault?
6. If a parent uses alcohol or drugs, it is their child's fault?
7. Why did Butch's Mom feel better at the end of the story?
8. Why did Butch feel better at the end of the story?

Name _____ Date_____

© 2008 RoboMedia, Inc. – www.LifeSkills4Kids.com

Healing Quiz

Dear Parent:

Please help your child complete the sentences below. This helps your child understand problems drugs can cause. Use each "Word Bank" word only once.

Word Bank

fault	drinks	help	addicted
alcohol	teacher	mind	different

1. Cigarettes, _____, marijuana, LSD and cocaine are all drugs.

2. Drugs change a person's body and _____.

3. When people use alcohol or other drugs, they may act _____.

4. If your friend's Dad _____ too much, your friend might feel bad because she thinks it's her fault.

5. It's not your friend's _____ if her dad drinks too much.

6. If a person feels sick when he stops taking a drug, he might be _____.

7. There are special doctors who can _____ people cure any drug problem.

8. If you have questions about drug problems, you can always ask your _____.

Answers: 1. alcohol 2. mind 3. different 4. drinks 5. fault 6. addicted 7. help 8. teacher

Name _____ Date _____

PARENT'S INITIALS

© Copyright 2008 RoboMedia, Inc. – www.LifeSkills4Kids.com

Earth Skills

18. I love my planet because it's special.

Lesson Notes: The *Million Dollar Machine* curriculum inspires children to respect themselves and others by demonstrating how special and precious people are. These "Earth Skills" lessons are a natural extension of this concept. This program's authors and educational consultants believe that developing healthy environmental attitudes will help your students develop healthy attitudes towards themselves. These activities explore the wonders of our planet Earth using the same techniques we used earlier to explore the wonders of the human body. Wikipedia article keywords are underlined for quick teacher reference.

Talk

- ☐ What "team" is every person a member of? **(The "Planet Earth Team.")**
- ☐ Where does *every* person on that "team" live?
- ☐ How is the planet Earth like your *Million Dollar Machine*?
  (e.g. we only get one, we're responsible for it, it's unique, it can fix itself sometimes, etc.)
- ☐ What are some things that make our planet special?
  (e.g. people live here, air, water, food, plants, animals, good temperature, etc.)
- ☐ How many planets do we get to live on?
- ☐ How many other planets are there?
- ☐ If we damage this planet, could we all move to another planet?
- ☐ What are some living things that share our planet with us?
- ☐ Are plants and animals parts of our team?
- ☐ What are natural resources?
  (e.g. natural products that the Earth has or produces like water, minerals, air, trees, etc.)
- ☐ Is there an unlimited amount of any natural resource?
- ☐ What would we do if we ran out of a natural resource?
- ☐ What are some things you like to do with your planet?
  (e.g. swim in the ocean, walk in the woods, climb trees, etc.)
- ☐ Why should we take good care of our planet?

Make

- ☐ **"Wonders of the World!"** Make a bulletin board divided into sections for "Natural Wonders of the World," "Animal Wonders of the World," "Plant Wonders of the World," "Mineral Wonders of the World," etc. Over a period of days or weeks, students can contribute drawings, photos, facts and stories related to each heading. You may wish to assign specific topics, require contributions on certain days or have students describe items to the class.

- ☐ **"Water, Water Everywhere"** Explain that water is the key to all life on Earth. Plants, animals and people need it to survive. Talk about how water changes from one form to another. **(e.g. humidity forming clouds, clouds forming rain, rain forming streams, etc.)** Have your students draw pictures of places that water is found. **(e.g. clouds, rain, sleet, snow, ice, streams, rivers, lakes, oceans, underground water, etc.)** Teacher Resource: Wikipedia articles on clouds, lakes, oceans, rivers, snow and water.

- ☐ **"Planet of Plenty"** Explain to students that plants produce most of the food that animals and humans eat. Have your class find or draw pictures of fruit and vegetable foods and make posters. Then, have each student draw a meal they would enjoy, using only the plant foods on the posters. Teacher Resources: Wikipedia articles on plants and food sources.

Earth Skills

- ☐ **"One in a Million"** Explain that Earth isn't the only planet in our Solar System but we couldn't live on other nearby planets because they don't have comfortable temperatures or enough water, air or food. Have students draw pictures of what a planet might look like if it was missing one or all of the important things that Earth has.
- ☐ **"Nature Museum"** Have each students bring in a natural object they found (e.g. seashell, rock, insect, plant, etc.) and learn a few facts about it. Have them describe their objects to the class and put the objects in a classroom display.
- ☐ **"What is It?"** Use the objects above to play a guessing game. Have a student think of one object and give descriptive clues to the class, one at a time. (e.g. Something used to live in it. It comes from the ocean. It has 2 halves. Etc.) The student who guesses the object first goes next.
- ☐ **"Home, Sweet Home!"** Have children make posters with this title. Have them decorate the poster with drawings or pictures related to something they love about the Earth.
- ☐ **"Landscape Artist"** Have children use modeling clay to create a scene from nature. They can include water, land, animals, etc.

Play

- ☐ **"Fresh Air"** Take your class outdoors to enjoy any of the "Talk" activities.
- ☐ **"I love my planet because..."** Take your class outdoors to sit in a circle. Have students take turns completing the sentence with something they love about the Earth.
- ☐ **"I spy..."** Take your class outdoors. Students pick a natural object and give descriptive clues. The rest of the class tries to guess the object.
- ☐ **"Nature's Names"** Take your class outdoors and sit in a circle. Tell your students to look around and think about nature. Have students name natural objects they can see (e.g. cloud, rock, grass, plant, puddle, tree, etc.) or natural objects that start with each letter of the alphabet. (e.g. Ant, Bird, Cat, Dog, Earth, Flower, Grass, Hill, etc.)
- ☐ **"World Travelers!"** Tell your children that they are going on a very exciting trip. They can choose to go to a jungle, a beach, a mountain, a desert, or the South Pole. Divide your class into groups. Have each group draw: things they would take to that place; how they would dress; and what they would like to do or see there. Then, have each group do a skit for the class about one adventure they might have.
- ☐ **"Picture a Plant"** Have each child draw a plant that benefits people in some way. (e.g. a plant that produces food, medicine, fabric, building materials, etc.) Students then show their drawings to the class and explain how the plant is useful.
- ☐ **"Adopt an Animal"** Explain that a "habitat" is where an animal or plant lives and grows. Have each child draw an animal or plant in its natural habitat.
- ☐ **"Resource Detective"** Have each child bring in an everyday object and report to the class which of the Earth's resources it is made from. (e.g. book – paper from trees; sandwich - cheese from cows, bread from wheat; etc.)
- ☐ **"Talking Earth"** Have your students make paper bag costumes decorated to look like one of the Earth's features. (e.g. trees, mountains, waterfalls, oceans, etc.) Students wear their costumes and tell the class how special their feature is.
- ☐ **"Visitor"** Invite a park ranger or naturalist to talk to your class about some of the wonderful aspects of nature. If possible, have them bring slides or photos.

Planet Quiz

Word Bank

food	oceans	jungle
Earth	air	recycling
one	conserve	water
	everyone's	

1. We only get _____ planet, so we have to take good care of it.

2. The name of our planet is _____.

3. Plants are important because they make the _____ we breathe.

4. Plants give us most of the _____ that we eat.

5. Most of the plants on our planet grow in the _____.

6. It's important for _____ to be clean because it keeps plants and animals alive, and we drink it.

7. Most of the water on our planet is in the _____.

8. To _____ means to use natural resources carefully.

9. When we use paper, glass, water, or aluminum over again, instead of throwing it away, that's called _____.

10. It's _____ job to take care of our planet.

PARENT'S INITIALS

Name _____

Date _____

© 2008 Copyright RoboMedia, Inc. – www.LifeSkills4Kids.com

I LOVE MY PLANET

Name _____
Date _____

PARENT'S INITIALS

You only get one Million Dollar Machine. That's why you take good care of it! We all share our planet and live together here. ***Did you ever think about how many planets we get?*** We only get one to share! So our planet is very special and we have to take care of it. Planet Earth has many beautiful parts. Color the picture and label the parts you know!

WORD BANK

air, tree, stream, cloud, people animals, birds, fish, mountain rain, sun, plants

© Copyright 2008 RoboMedia, Inc. – www.LifeSkills4Kids.com

Earth Skills

19. I'm an important member of nature's team.

Lesson Notes: These activities help children understand that they are an important part of a global ecosystem that includes people, animals, plants and resources. The first goal is to give children a clear sense of belonging to the world they see around them. The second goal is to demonstrate that things in the world affect each other. Finally, these activities empower children with the knowledge that they can exert a positive influence on their surroundings. Many activities can be related to Interpersonal Skills Lessons 5, 6, 7, 8 and 9. Wikipedia article keywords are underlined for quick teacher reference.

Talk

- ☐ Are people part of nature or different from nature?
- ☐ Tell about a time when the weather affected you.
  (e.g. snow canceled school, rain made a rainbow, swam on hot day, etc.)
- ☐ What other living things do we share our planet with?
- ☐ What are some smart animals that live on the planet Earth?
- ☐ How do people affect other animals on Earth?
- ☐ Do we have a responsibility to help other animals?
- ☐ Tell about a time that you helped an animal.
- ☐ Do we have a responsibility to keep our planet clean?
- ☐ What would happen if everyone littered just a little bit?
- ☐ How does littering hurt people and animals?
- ☐ What happens to garbage when we throw it away?
- ☐ What happens to dirty water when it goes down the drain?
- ☐ Where does our drinking water come from?
- ☐ Where does the air we breathe come from?
- ☐ Where does our food come from?
- ☐ How do air and water affect the food we eat?

Make

- ☐ **"Down the Drain"** As a class project, find out where clean water comes from and where it goes when it goes down the drain. Make a bulletin board display of the water cycle.
  (e.g. evaporation, clouds, rain, ground water, well, etc.)
- ☐ **"A Place for Everything"** Have your students name some fun things to do outdoors. **(e.g. walk in the woods, climb mountains, swim at the beach, canoe on streams, etc.)** Have students draw pictures of themselves enjoying one of the activities.
- ☐ **"Fun in the Sun!"** Have your children draw their favorite outdoor activities **(e.g. swimming, climbing trees, flying a kite, playing ball, etc.)** or places **(e.g. waterfall, woods, snow, etc.)**. Have them present their finished scenes to the class and tell how important clean air, water and land are to enjoying their activity.
- ☐ **"America the Beautiful"** Have your students find some litter near their home or school and draw a picture of it. Then, they should clean up the litter and draw the same scene again, without the litter. Divide a bulletin board into "Before" and "After" sections. Put the litter drawings on one side and the drawings of a clean environment on the other.

Earth Skills

- ☐ **"Animal's Best Friend"** Have your students draw pictures of a person taking care of a pet or animal. **(e.g. feeding, walking, playing, etc.)** Display the drawings and talk about how pets depend on us for care. Discuss how other animals depend on human kindness.
- ☐ **"Forever is a Long Time"** Explain that some things people do, like building cities, can destroy the places that animals live. Sometimes, these things cause a type of animal to disappear entirely. This is called <u>extinction</u>. When an animal is extinct, it is gone forever. As a class project, learn about some animals that are close to extinction and draw them. **(e.g. <u>elephants</u>, <u>whales</u>, <u>manatees</u>, etc.)** Find out what people are doing to help these animals.

Play

- ☐ **"Friendship Tree"** Make a tree outline on a bulletin board. Have children trace their hands on green construction paper, cut out the tracings, sign them and glue them to the branches like leaves. Discuss how we are each unique and special, yet still part of the classroom group. Relate that concept to how we are all part of nature, too.
- ☐ **"Classroom Garden"** Explain to students that <u>plants</u> are our friends on Earth. They make the air we breathe and we make the air they breathe. Plants also need water, food and sunshine just like we do. As a class project, have students sprout, buy or bring in some plants to grow (<u>beans</u> and <u>Nasturtiums</u> are hardy). Have students take turns caring for the plants. Plants don't always adapt to classroom life so avoid disappointments by not assigning plants to individual students.
- ☐ **"Spring has Sprung"** In the Spring, sprout flower seeds and plant them around your school.
- ☐ **"Soft Scene"** Have your students cut out pieces of fabric shaped like objects from nature. **(e.g. clouds, mountains, birds, trees, plants, people, etc.)** They can use the shapes to create nature scenes on a flannel board. You might use the scene on the worksheet as a start. Have students describe how the objects in each scene could affect each other.
- ☐ **"Better Listen!"** Have your students pretend to be parts of the environment. **(e.g. park, ocean, lake, forest, back yard, etc.)** The "environment" then talks to humans about how it is being treated. **(e.g. Ocean: "Hey! Quit dumping garbage in me! It stinks!" or Park: "Thank you for taking care of me and planting all those pretty trees!" Etc.)**
- ☐ **"The Giving Tree"** *'Once there was a tree...and she loved a little boy.'* So begins an unforgettable story of perception, beautifully written and illustrated by the gifted author Shel Silverstein. Read this book to your class. Then, read the story again as half the students play the tree's role and half play the boy. **(Harper & Row, ISBN 978-0060256654)**
- ☐ **"Visitor"** Invite someone from the sanitation department to discuss where trash goes, how much it costs to keep your town clean and who pays for it. If recycling is available, have your guest describe the process. If recycling is not available, have your guest explain why.
- ☐ Consult **"The Kid's Guide to Service Projects - Over 500 Service Ideas for Young People Who Want to Make a Difference" by Barbara Lewis, ISBN 978-0915793822**, for an excellent selection of student activities related to caring for the environment and for other people.

Life Cycles

Things in our world affect each other all the time. By coloring the picture below, you'll see how some things in our world can affect each other.

After you're done, answer the questions with a parent.

A *cycle* is when one thing affects another thing, and *that* affects the first thing. If you're nice to your friend, your friend will be nice to you When your friend is nice to you, you want to be even nicer to your friend. That's a *cycle*!

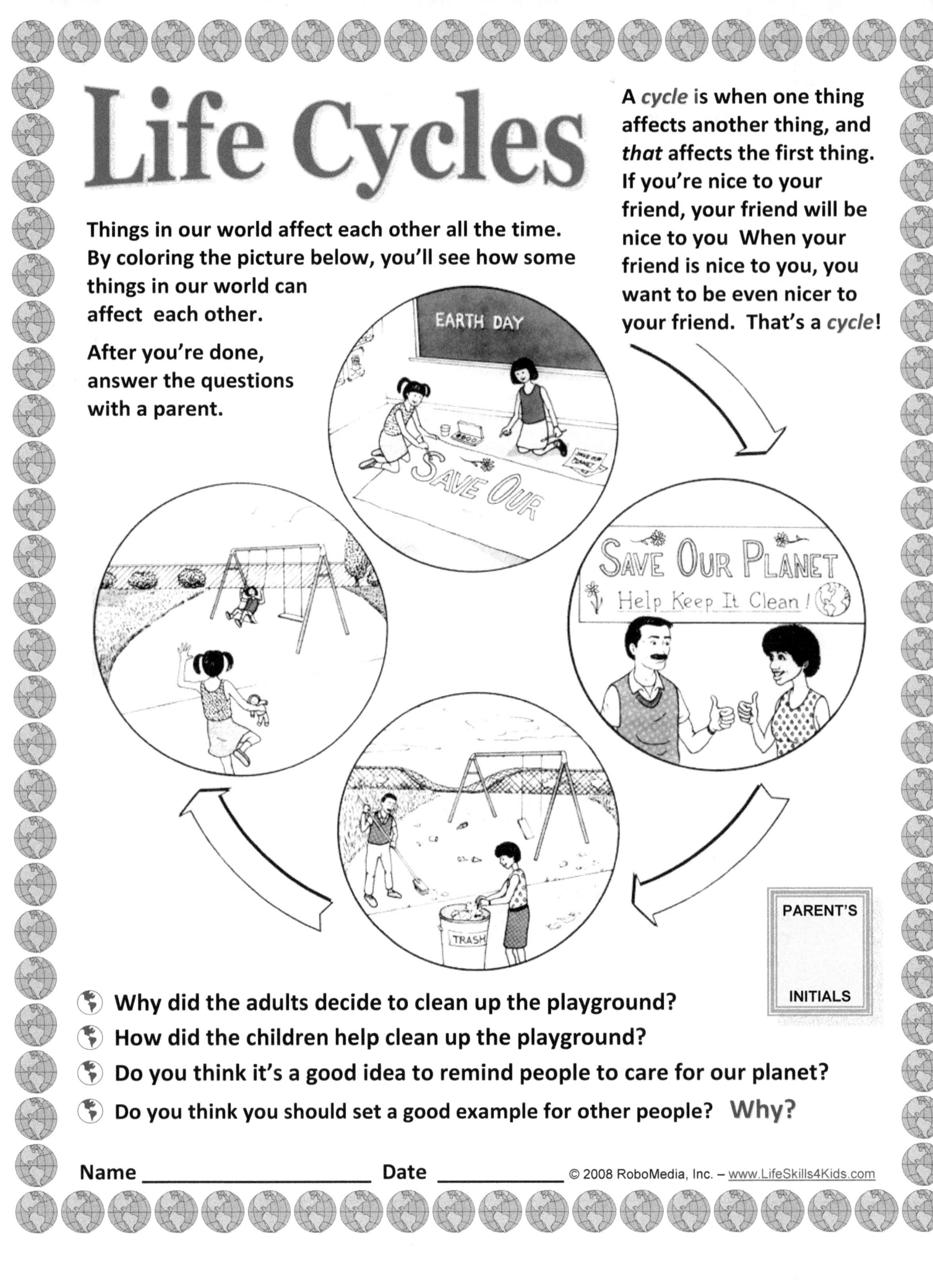

- 🌎 Why did the adults decide to clean up the playground?
- 🌎 How did the children help clean up the playground?
- 🌎 Do you think it's a good idea to remind people to care for our planet?
- 🌎 Do you think you should set a good example for other people? **Why?**

PARENT'S INITIALS

Name _____ Date _____ © 2008 RoboMedia, Inc. – www.LifeSkills4Kids.com

SHARING ONE WORLD

People are an important part of nature. We all share the Earth. We all do things that affect other people and our planet. That's because everything is connected.

If you smile at someone . . . and make them feel good, they may smile at someone else and make *them* happy. **Your smile gets passed on!** If you pick up some litter, someone might copy your good deed and pick up some litter too. And the world we share gets a little cleaner! But if people make the world dirty, that gets passed along too. **Color the picture below and discuss the questions with a parent.**

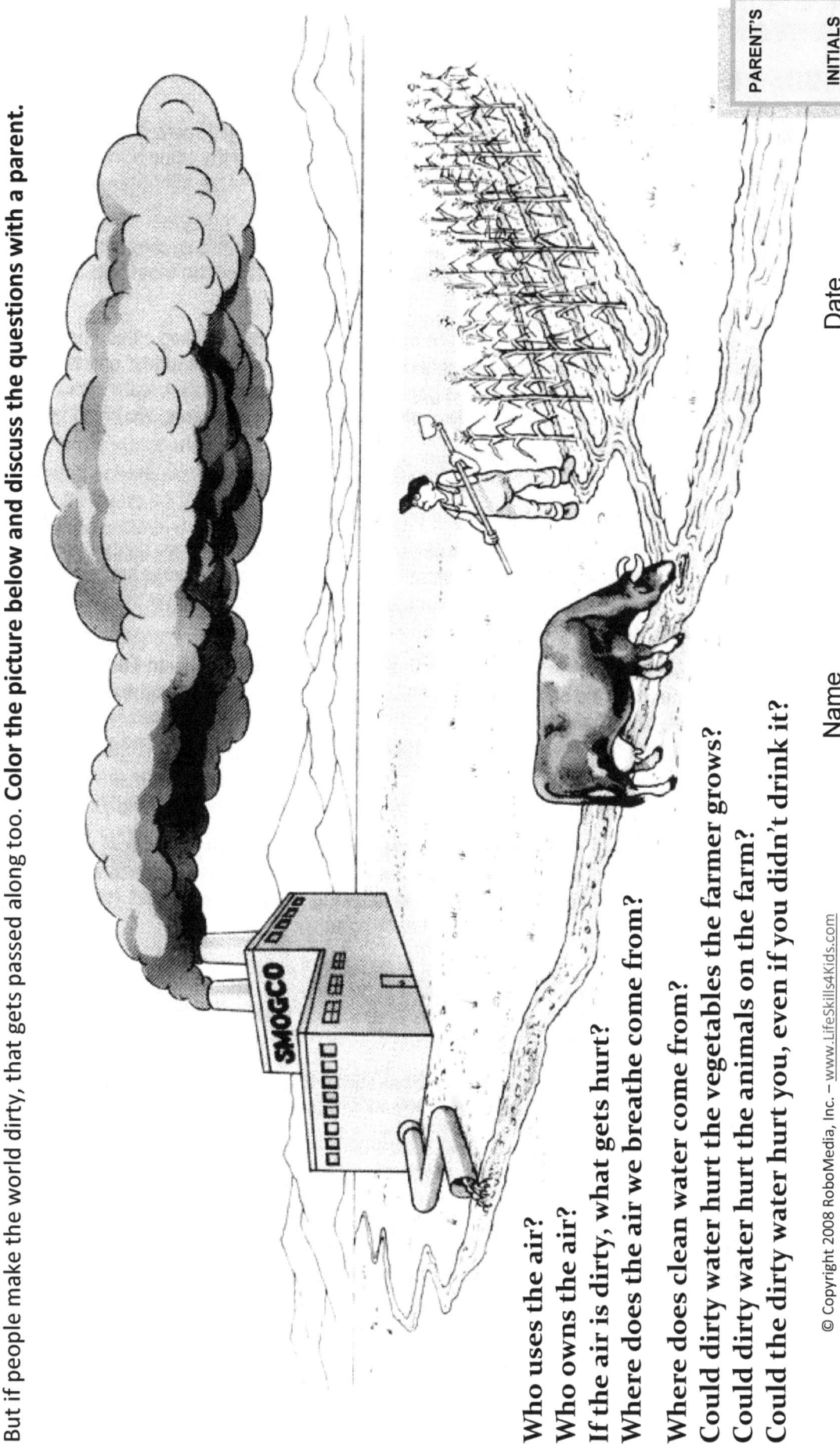

Who uses the air?
Who owns the air?
If the air is dirty, what gets hurt?
Where does the air we breathe come from?

Where does clean water come from?
Could dirty water hurt the vegetables the farmer grows?
Could dirty water hurt the animals on the farm?
Could the dirty water hurt you, even if you didn't drink it?

Name _____ Date _____

PARENT'S INITIALS

© Copyright 2008 RoboMedia, Inc. – www.LifeSkills4Kids.com

Interpersonal Skills

20. I help keep my planet clean and healthy.

Lesson Notes: These activities help children develop ecologically healthy habits and skills. Even the youngest children can begin to understand conservation concepts and learn to practice environmentally beneficial behaviors. The goal is to inspire children to participate in positive global efforts to improve our environment and to give them the skills to do so. Wikipedia article keywords are underlined for quick teacher reference.

Talk

- ☐ What are some of the ways the Earth takes care of you?
  (e.g. gives you air, warmth, food, gravity, protection from the sun, water, etc.)
- ☐ Whose job is it to take care of the planet Earth?
- ☐ Can young people do things to help the Earth, too?
- ☐ What are some things you can do to make a difference?
- ☐ How can you get other people to help you take care of the planet?
- ☐ Why do we try to keep our home, school and community clean?
- ☐ How do you feel when you see someone throwing trash on the ground?
- ☐ What would happen if everyone littered just a little bit?
- ☐ If you always throw your trash away properly, do you think other people might copy you?
- ☐ What does it mean to conserve something? **(to use something wisely, without wasting it)**
- ☐ Why is it important to conserve some things? (See Wikipedia keyword conservation ethic)
- ☐ What are some things we can conserve?
  (water, electricity, gasoline, natural gas, paper products)
- ☐ What does recycling mean? **(to reuse an item or the material that it is made of)**
- ☐ Why is recycling important?
- ☐ What are some things we can recycle? **(aluminum, glass, paper, plastic)**
- ☐ What are some things we can donate? **(clothes, books, toys)**
- ☐ What are some hazardous waste items we must dispose of properly? **(paint, chemicals, oil, garbage)**

Make

- ☐ **"Around He Goes!"** Write a class story about recycling starring a fictional character like "Al the Aluminum Can" or "Nancy the Newspaper." Trace the character's history from raw material, through manufacture and use, to recycling. Talk about how recycling gives the character a chance to be useful again.
- ☐ **"Recycle Me!"** Have your students make a display of items that can be recycled and items that are made from recycled materials.
- ☐ **"Dream Machine"** Have your students create imaginary inventions that do things to help the environment. (e.g. air cleaning machine, endangered species protector, recycling machine, water purifier, etc.) Have them draw their machines or build them with cardboard tubes, spools of thread and other trash items. Then, have them present their creations to the class, explaining why they think an invention like theirs would be a good thing.

Interpersonal Skills

- ☐ **"Reusable or Disposable?"** Explain to your students that items we use again and again are reusable. **(e.g. glass plates, cloth diapers, towels, etc.)** Items we use only once are disposable. **(e.g. paper plates, paper diapers, paper towels, etc.)** The problem with disposable items is that they turn into trash after only one use. Have students draw 3 disposable items and 3 reusable items that they have at home. Hold a class discussion about how they could replace disposable items with reusable items.

- ☐ **"I Keep It Clean"** Have your students describe things they do to take care of the planet. **(e.g. plant flowers, recycle bottles, pick up litter, turn off water, turn off lights, etc.)** List these on the chalkboard. Have students draw their favorite individually or in groups.

- ☐ **"The Earth Needs YOU!"** Have your students make inspirational posters showing conservation tips. Draw ideas from the "I'm a Conservation Helper" worksheet. Display the posters in a public place like the library, mall, grocery store, town hall, etc.

- ☐ **"Barrels of Fun"** Have your students decorate trash bins to use in a recycling project. Put the bins in the lunch room to collect cans, bottles and paper. Check with your local city hall to find out who can reuse the collected materials.

Play

- ☐ **"Don't be a Litterbug"** Discuss why it's important to put litter in its place. Divide the class into groups and have them compete to see who can collect the most litter. Have a picnic lunch in the clean park when you're done. Visit the LitterItCostsYou.org website for ideas.

- ☐ **"Remember What to Recycle"** Have students gather a collection of 10-15 items that can be recycled. **(e.g. 6 bottles, 6 cans, 3 newspapers)** and take turns removing or adding one object while the rest of the class hides their eyes. Students try to guess what is missing or what is new.

- ☐ **"Class Tree"** Ask a local nursery to donate a small tree **(2-3 feet high)** for your class to plant at school. Everyone can work together to decide where to plant it, dig the hole, water it, etc.

- ☐ **"Fantastic Family"** Have your students ask their parents for an example of what their family does to conserve resources. **(e.g. reuse paper bags, install low volume shower heads, turn down hot water heater, ride bikes on errands, etc.)** Have students draw a picture of the activity and explain it to the class. Resource: Teachers can visit Conservation International at Conservation.org for more ideas on ecologically friendly "green living" and proactive projects for students.

- ☐ **"Paper Drive"** Organize an aluminum recycling, plastic recycling or paper recycling drive. Explain that the Earth's resources are limited. By recycling we can use the same material again and again. If money can be raised through the drive, use it to fund a nature study field trip, tree planting, etc.

- ☐ **"Excuse Me But..."** Divide your class into groups to role play situations where a friend, parent or stranger is littering, wasting energy, etc. Students must politely explain why we shouldn't do these things.

- ☐ **"Visitor"** Invite a conservationist to talk to your class about what they can do to keep the Earth clean and healthy. Ask them about local projects that young people can participate in.

I'm a Conservation Helper!

Here are things you can do to keep your planet healthy!
Check (✓) each one you are able to do.

- ☐ **Save energy!** Turn off the TV if no one is watching it.
- ☐ Turn off lights when you leave a room, even for 10 minutes.

Save Resources

- ☐ Reuse paper bags to save trees **or** get reusable bags.
- ☐ Recycle newspapers, aluminum cans, plastic and glass bottles.
- ☐ Turn off the water when brushing your teeth.

Be a Conservation helper!

☐ With your parent, write a letter to the President! Ask him to give you a clean, pollution-free world to grow up in! Here is the President's address:

> President _____
> The White House
> 1600 Pennsylvania Ave.
> Washington D.C. 20500

☐ Don't litter. Pick up trash when you see it. This will inspire other people, too!

☐ Plant a tree, bush, flowers or vegetables at your house.

☐ Practice these conservation tips yourself to set a good example for others.

Name _____ Date _____

PARENT'S INITIALS

© Copyright 2008 RoboMedia, Inc. – www.LifeSkills4Kids.com

Use it Wisely!

Our planet's gifts to us are called *natural resources*.

Our job is to use Earth's gifts *wisely* without wasting them.

Help PJ decide the wisest ways to use the resources pictured on the left. Draw a line from each item to the best use.

Water

CONSERVE
Don't use too much!

Books

Gas

Newspapers

DONATE
Give it to someone else to use

Clothes

Electricity

RECYCLE
Use the material over again!

Toys

Glass & Cans

When you're done, discuss these questions with your family.
- Why is it a good idea not to waste electricity and water?
- How do we save money by conserving things?
- What kind of useful things can we donate to other people?
- Why is donating things we don't need a nice thing to do?
- Does our town have a recycling center?
- Does our family recycle anything?

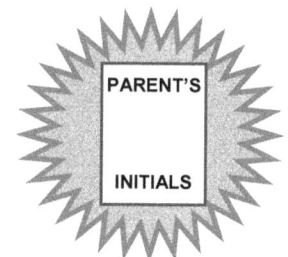
PARENT'S INITIALS

Name _____ Date _____

© 2008 RoboMedia, Inc. – www.LifeSkills4Kids.com

Vocabulary K-3

Note to Teacher: These words are drawn from the 20 Learning Objectives. Familiarizing your students with them will enable you to conduct more thorough discussions. Challenge your students with some of the following activities:

- Hold a Million Dollar Machine Spelling Bee.
- Have students make up a Million Dollar Machine version of "Pictionary."
- Use them as Million Dollar Machine Bonus Words on regular spelling tests.
- Have students pantomime words from specific Learning Objectives.
- Have students use them in a sentence or statement as a "Word of the Day" activity.

Learning Objective 1.
individual
irreplaceable
love
personal
possession
priceless
special
strength
unique
weakness

Learning Objective 2.
angry
confused
embarrassed
express
feelings
guess
happy
remind
upset
worry

Learning Objective 3.
appearance
benefits
exercise
expensive
food
healthy
important
nutritious
rest
valuable

Learning Objective 4.
achieve
certificate
create
fail
goal
ideal
improve
opportunity
reward
succeed

Learning Objective 5.
common
different
difficult
handicap
introduce
qualities
similarities
signature
social
talent

Learning Objective 6.
compliment
courtesy
fragile
helpful
kindness
manners
polite
property
respect
share

Learning Objective 7.
citizen
community
contribution
cooperation
harmony
rules
spirit
team
teamwork
unity

Learning Objective 8.
empathy
friend
friendship
generous
humor
neighborhood
patience
reaction
recipe
sensitive

Learning Objective 9.
baby
family
favorite
job
member
portrait
privacy
relative
responsibilities
together

K-3 Vocabulary

Learning Objective 10.
advertisement
caring
choice
decision
habit
interesting
prevent
problem
solve
wrong

Learning Objective 11.
avoid
choose
compare
consequence
judge
list
negative
positive
recognize
solution

Learning Objective 12.
avoid
influence
lie
pressure
peer pressure
resist
rights
safe
trouble
unsafe

Learning Objective 13.
advice
emergency
experience
helper
guidance
ordinarily
professional
stranger
suspicious
trust

Learning Objective 14.
accident
cautious
dangerous
illegal
improperly
poison
protect
risk
substance
toxic

Learning Objective 15.
alcohol
alternatives
cancer
defense
drugs
fatal
harmful
permission
tobacco
warning

Learning Objective 16.
disease
doctor
dosage
imbalance
ingestion
medicine
non-prescription
prescription
supervision
vaccine

Learning Objective 17.
addiction
alcoholism
chore
dependence
encourage
gentle
healing
fault
realize
specialist

Learning Objective 18.
appreciate
atmosphere
Earth
mineral
nature
natural
planet
resource
unlimited
wonder

Learning Objective 19.
animal
cycle
environment
extinction
garbage
habitat
restore
sanitation
waste
weather

Learning Objective 20.
conservation
conserve
consume
dispose
donate
eliminate
hazardous
landfill
litter
recycle

For Online Learning Resources visit:
www.LifeSkills4Kids.com

Make your Life Skills and Character Education lessons even more effective and fun with our online resources:

LifeSkills4kids.com — Helping children achieve their *personal best since 1986*

- ✓ **Life Skills Lesson Plans** - Order our Life Skills Lesson Collections in three convenient formats: Digital Download, Printed Books and DVD.
- ✓ **FREE Lesson Samples** - Your friends can try our lessons with free downloads.
- ✓ **Program Validation** - Get complete details on scientific studies by Columbia University and the University of Medicine that validate our Life Skills lessons.
- ✓ **Educator Comments** - Find out what teachers, parents and community leaders across the USA think about the Million Dollar Machine Program.
- ✓ **School Assembly Program with Robot Teacher** - Find out how to have our amazing robot life skills teacher visit your child's school.
- ✓ **Robot Teacher Video** - See our robot teacher in the classroom.
- ✓ **Life Skills Store** - Books, games and products for children and adults.
- ✓ **Life Skills Knowledge Base** - A growing collection of free articles with ideas, guest columnists, books and Internet resources.

Sample articles from our free *Life Skills Knowledge Base*:

1. Dealing with Bullies
- ✓ Welcome: "Dealing with Bullies"
- ✓ Feature: "Tips to deal with bullying behavior"
- ✓ Teacher/Parent Book: "The Bully Free Classroom"
- ✓ K-3 Book: "The Ant Bully"
- ✓ 4-6 Book: "Taking the Bully by the Horns"
- ✓ Web Discoveries: "Stop the Bullies"
- ✓ Words of Wisdom: "Bully behavior-Peaceful quotes"

2. Outdoor Activities with Kids
- ✓ Welcome: "Kids and the Great Outdoors"
- ✓ Feature: "Get Back to Nature With Your Kids"
- ✓ Book Pick: "Wild Days: Discovery Journals"
- ✓ K-3 Book: "Outdoor Survival Handbook for Kids"
- ✓ K-3 Book: "The Kids Campfire Book"
- ✓ 4-6 Book: "Essential Camping for Teens"
- ✓ Web Discoveries: "Outdoor recreation websites"
- ✓ Words of Wisdom: "Getting back to Nature"

3. Rural Lessons for Suburban Kids
- ✓ Feature: "Community Service in Appalachia"
- ✓ Teacher/Parent Book: "Hunter's Horn"
- ✓ K-3 Book: "When I Was Young in the Mountains"
- ✓ K-3 Book: "Mama is a Miner"
- ✓ 4-6 Book: "Rocket Boys; A Memoir"
- ✓ 4-6 Book: "American Folktales and Songs"
- ✓ Web Discoveries: "Habitat For Humanity"
- ✓ Words of Wisdom: "Turn of the Century Kids"

4. Children and Obesity
- ✓ Welcome: "When are kids (and adults) too FAT?"
- ✓ Feature: "Ten Tips for Thinner Kids"
- ✓ Teacher/Parent Book: "How to teach kids nutrition."
- ✓ Teacher/Parent Book: "Fast Food Nation"
- ✓ K-3 Book: "The Edible Pyramid"
- ✓ K-3 Book: "The Great Cupcake Caper"
- ✓ 4-6 Book: "Good Enough to Eat"
- ✓ 4-6 Book: "The Race Against Junkfood"
- ✓ Web Discoveries: "KidsFood Cyber Club"
- ✓ Words of Wisdom: "Food, glorious food!"

5. Moderation, Simplicity and Fulfillment
- Welcome: "Less TV + More Talk = Better Kids"
- Feature: "Tests a poor substitute for good parenting"
- Teacher/Parent Book: "Stop Teaching Kids to Kill"
- K-3 Book: "Madlenka"
- 4-6 Book: "A Wrinkle in Time"
- Web Discoveries: " Institute on Media and Family"
- Words of Wisdom: "Time - Our priceless resource"

6. Children and TV
- Welcome: "Moderation, simplicity and fulfillment"
- Feature: "Make a promise to your children"
- Teacher/Parent Book: "Simplify Life With Kids"
- K-3 Book: "Because Brian Hugged His Mother"
- 4-6 Book: "Ramona the Brave"
- Web Discoveries: "Center for a New American Dream"
- Words of Wisdom: "Less is More"

7. Reading Skills
- Welcome: "Reading - A life skill that's always in style!"
- Feature: "A book speaks"
- Book Pick: "Teaching Kids to Care & Cooperate"
- K-3 Book: "Lucky the Golden Goose"
- 4-6 Book: "Harriet the Spy"
- Web Discoveries: "Best reading & book sites"
- Words of Wisdom: "Three cures for kid's boredom"

8. Teaching Children to be Teachers
- Welcome: "Who Wants to be a Teacher?"
- Feature: "The Passion for Teaching"
- Teacher/Parent Book: "The One Minute Teacher"
- K-3 Book: "One of Each"
- 4-6 Book: "A Leader's Guide to I Like Being Me"
- Web Discoveries: "Igniting Your Natural Genius"
- Words of Wisdom: "Sharing the gift of Knowledge"

9. Volunteerism - Growing by Giving
- Welcome: "Volunteerism - Growing by giving"
- Feature: "How to be a Local Hero"
- Book - "500 Service Ideas for Young People"
- K-3 Book: "Berenstain Bears and Those in Need"
- K-3 Book: "How We Made the World a Better Place"
- 4-6 Book: "Kid's Guide to Social Action"
- Web Discoveries: "How to donate valuable time"
- Words of Wisdom: "The spirit of contribution"

10. Character Education
- Welcome: "Character Ed-A key life skills component"
- Feature: "The five "W's" of Character Education"
- Teacher/Parent Book: "K-6 Character Education"
- K-3 Book: "If you had to choose, what would you do?"
- 4-6 Book: "A Call to Character - A Family Treasury"
- Web Discoveries: "Character Education on the web"
- Words of Wisdom: "From some famous characters"

11. Back to School Tips
- Welcome: "Back to school? Already???"
- Feature: "In the face of frustration"
- Teacher/Parent Book: "If you don't feed the teachers..."
- K-3 Book: "I don't want to go back to school!"
- 4-6 Book: "American Heritage Children's Dictionary"
- Web Discoveries: "Back to School Websites"
- Words of Wisdom: "Kids Do's & Don'ts for Dads"

12. Parenting Skills & Active Parenting
- Welcome: "Activate your parenting skills!"
- Feature: "Active Parenting-Teaching Responsibility"
- Teacher/Parent Book: "Go to Your Room! "
- K-3 Book: "Pierre; a Cautionary Tale "
- 4-6 Book: "Charlie and the Chocolate Factory"
- Web Discoveries: "Top Parenting Websites"
- Words of Wisdom: "Courage and Fear"

13. Children and the Internet
- Welcome: "Guest columnists, poets & web travelers!"
- Feature: "The promise of the computer age"
- Teacher/Parent Book: "Boundaries for Kids"
- K-3 Book: "Poetry Anthologies for Children"
- 4-6 Book: "Earthwatch"
- Web Discoveries: "Your Virtual Passport to the World"
- Words of Wisdom: "A Parent's Wish for Her Children"

14. Children and Media
- Welcome: "Meet the Press!"
- Editorial: "Play Station Education?"
- Feature: "Make bad news better - 5 easy steps!"
- Teacher/Parent Book: "Measure of Our Success"
- K-3 Book: "The Giving Tree"
- 4-6 Book: "Holes"
- Web Discoveries: "TV, Radio & Reporters on the Web"
- Words of Wisdom: "All the news (quotes) fit to print"

15. Life Skills Teaching Techniques
- Welcome: Can you help life skills interest grow?
- Feature: "How do your children learn?
- 6 great teaching techniques!"
- Teacher/Parent Book: "Parenting with Love & Logic"
- K-3 Book: "1,000 Years Ago on Planet Earth"
- 4-6 Book: "Weslandia"
- Web Discoveries: "Spring FITNESS Fun for Kids!"
- Words of Wisdom: "Children Learn What They Live"

16. Talking With Your Children
- Feature: "Life skills talk is cheap . . . And effective!"
- Teacher/Parent Book: "Home Comforts"
- K-3 Book: "Beetle Boy"
- 4-6 Book: "Bud, Not Buddy!"
- Web Discoveries: "3 great NUTRITION sites!"
- Words of Wisdom: "IMAGINATION, the spark of life"

17. Kids & Tobacco
- Feature: "Up in Smoke? Kids & Tobacco"
- Teacher/Parent Book: "Lanterns"
- K-3 Book: "Nova's Ark"
- 4-6 Book: "The New Way Things Work"
- Web Discoveries: for teachers, parents & kids
- Words of Wisdom: "Henry Ford's ideas on success"

MDM Program Facts

- The Million Dollar Machine Program (MDM) is a comprehensive life skills enrichment curriculum that teaches children a variety of personal, social, health and environmental skills to help them achieve their personal best in life.

- The MDM lessons include character education, decision making techniques and assertiveness skills that inspire children to avoid risky behaviors, including the use of cigarettes, alcohol and other drugs.

- MDM is recommended for all children in Elementary Grades K-6 (ages 5-11). More than 3,000,000 children have experienced the MDM assembly in their schools.

- In school programs, students, teachers and parents learn the MDM concepts in a dynamic live assembly: an interactive, multi-media robot teacher conducts the entire 40 minute presentation. There, <u>children learn that their bodies, not the robot, are the real "million dollar machines" for which the program is named</u>.

- The MDM lesson collection includes more than 1,200 integrated activities and discussion topics, 80 interactive parent/child worksheets and complete implementation guidelines. Regional programs can include posters, newsletters and other educational supplements.

- Five scientific studies by Columbia University, the University of Medicine & Dentistry New Jersey, and Vanderveer Research Group of Atlanta validate MDM's effectiveness showing: improved student skills and attitudes; greater happiness and self worth; excellent retention; and a decrease in actual and potential drug use. The research demonstrates an extremely high level of teacher and student satisfaction with MDM and its curriculum materials.

- Endorsement letters on file from thousands of educators, government officials, parents and children praise MDM, most often noting its "innovative method of instruction," "lasting positive influence," "high quality learning materials," and the "enthusiasm shown by participating teachers, parents, and children."

- State Governors in New Jersey, Ohio, Maryland, California, Texas and Florida have formally recognized MDM's positive influence. Mayors in major cities including Cincinnati, Dallas, Indianapolis, Memphis, Miami, New Orleans, and San Antonio have proclaimed "Million Dollar Machine Weeks" recognizing MDM's benefits.

- MDM sponsors have received millions of dollars worth of positive media coverage. Television news programs featuring MDM include CNN, Good Morning America, the Today Show, and hundreds of local NBC, CBS and ABC affiliates.

- President Bush recognized MDM with a Presidential Award for Private Sector Initiatives at the White house in 1989. MDM was also nominated for a Presidential Point of Light Award.

- Foundations, corporations and grants fund MDM in many schools as a highly visible community service. The complete program costs districts less than $3 per student.

To bring MDM to your district, please call Jeanne Burckhardt at 800-262-2162
For more information, please visit our website:
www.LifeSkills4Kids.com

www.ingramcontent.com/pod-product-compliance
Lightning Source LLC
Chambersburg PA
CBHW081202020426
42333CB00020B/2593